Slim&Trim
Cookbook

Slim&Trim
Cookbook

Slim&Trim
Cookbook

Slim&Trim
Cookbook

Slim&Trim
Cookbook

Slim&Trim
Cookbook

Slim&Trim
Cookbook

Slim&Trim
Cookbook

Slim&Trim
Cookbook

Slim&Trim
Cookbook

Slim&Trim
Cookbook

Slim&Trim
Cookbook

Slim&Trim
Cookbook

Slim&Trim
Cookbook

Slim&Trim
Cookbook

Slim&Trim
Cookbook

Slim&Trim
Cookbook

Slim&Trim
Cookbook

Consultant Nutritionist Jenny Salmon MSc BSc SRD AIFST

HAMLYN
London·New York·Sydney·Toronto

Acknowledgements

Edited by Carol Bowen
Photography by Paul Williams
Page 1 shows Stuffed Pepper (see page 44)
Page 2 shows Seafood Special (see page 43)
Illustrations by Marilyn Day

The recipes in this book have been created by the following companies:—

Cadbury Typhoo Limited
P.O. Box 171, Franklin House, Bournville,
Birmingham, B30 2NA

Hermes Sweeteners Limited
5 Langley Street, London WC2 9JA

Slimcea Limited
New Malden House, 1 Blagdon Road, New Malden,
Surrey, KT3 4TB

Van den Berghs and Jurgens Limited 1981
Sussex House, Civic Way, Burgess Hill, West Sussex

and coordinated in the kitchens of the Hamlyn Publishing Group.

Published by
The Hamlyn Publishing Group Limited
London · New York · Sydney · Toronto
Astronaut House, Feltham, Middlesex, England

ISBN 0 600 32229 7

Filmset by Photocomp Limited, Birmingham
Printed in Spain by
Printer, industria gráfica sa   Barcelona
D.L.B. 38345-1980

Contents

Useful facts and figures

Notes on metrication

In this book quantities are given in metric and Imperial measures. Exact conversion from Imperial to metric measures does not usually give very convenient working quantities and so the metric measures have been rounded off into units of 25 grams. The table below shows the recommended equivalents.

Ounces	Approx. g to nearest whole figure	Recommended conversion to nearest unit of 25
1	28	25
2	57	50
3	85	75
4	113	100
5	142	150
6	170	175
7	198	200
8	227	225
9	255	250
10	283	275
11	312	300
12	340	350
13	368	375
14	396	400
15	425	425
16 (1 lb)	454	450
17	482	475
18	510	500
19	539	550
20 (1¼ lb)	567	575

Note: When converting quantities over 20 oz first add the appropriate figures in the centre column, then adjust to the nearest unit of 25. As a general guide, 1 kg (1000 g) equals 2.2 lb or about 2 lb 3 oz. This method of conversion gives good results in nearly all cases, although in certain pastry and cake recipes a more accurate conversion is necessary to produce a balanced recipe.

Liquid measures. The millilitre has been used in this book and the following table gives a few examples.

Imperial	Approx. ml to nearest whole figure	Recommended ml
¼ pint	142	150 ml
½ pint	283	300 ml
¾ pint	425	450 ml
1 pint	567	600 ml
1½ pints	851	900 ml
1¾ pints	992	1000 ml (1 litre)

Spoon measures. All spoon measures in this book are level unless otherwise stated.

Can sizes. At present, cans are marked with the exact (usually to the nearest number) metric equivalent of the Imperial weight of the contents, so we have followed this practice when giving can sizes.

Oven temperatures

The table below gives recommended equivalents.

	°C	°F	Gas mark
Very cool	110	225	¼
	120	250	½
Cool	140	275	1
	150	300	2
Moderate	160	325	3
	180	350	4
Moderately hot	190	375	5
	200	400	6
Hot	220	425	7
	230	450	8
Very hot	240	475	9

NOTE: WHEN MAKING ANY OF THE RECIPES IN THIS BOOK, ONLY FOLLOW ONE SET OF MEASURES AS THEY ARE NOT INTERCHANGEABLE.

Introduction

Cadbury's Marvel is an instant low fat skimmed milk powder made from pure fresh milk, to the very highest possible standards of quality. Almost all the fat is removed from the milk leaving the proteins, minerals and water-soluble vitamins. The liquid is dried and 'instantised' to form easily reconstituted granules. Liquid Marvel has about 200 Calories per 568 ml (1 pint) compared with 400 Calories in whole milk. Marvel can be used for all beverages and in cooking, as a powder or liquid.

Hermesetas Liquid Sweetener is useful for sweetening creamy or fluid desserts, stewed fruit, jellies, etc., and for sweetening cold drinks. One teaspoon of Hermesetas Liquid Sweetener has the sweetening strength of 50 g/2 oz sugar and only 3.8 Calories.

Hermesetas Sprinkle Sweet looks like granulated sugar and, spoon for spoon, gives the same sweetness as sugar, but it is much lighter than sugar and contains only a tenth of the calories of sugar. Thus a tablespoon of ordinary sugar has about 60 Calories but a tablespoon of Sprinkle Sweet has only 6 Calories.

Hermesetas Tablets are completely calorie free and are useful for sweetening hot drinks such as tea and coffee. One Hermesetas Tablet has the sweetening strength of two small sugar lumps or one good teaspoon of sugar.

Outline is a low fat spread. Because it contains more water than butter or margarine it has fewer calories. 25 g/1 oz Outline has about 105 Calories compared with 210 Calories in butter and margarine. Outline has the same amounts of vitamins A and D as margarine (more than butter). Its main use is as a spread for bread.

Slimcea bread has only 35 Calories per slice compared with 51 per equal slice of ordinary bread. It can be used in exactly the same way as ordinary bread and is available in white or brown.

If you're about to have yet another go at slimming or you're a new recruit, take heart from the fact that there are a few more people doing precisely the same as you. In fact, there are probably a few million in this country alone. It's estimated that, every year, about 11 million people try to lose weight – that is about a fifth of the total population. When the other members of your family, even your friends, try to convince you you're not fat, you're meant to be that (round) shape, that you'll look old and haggard if you lose even a few pounds – remember the other millions who are going through the same experience. You're not alone in the battle!

Just knowing that there are many more slimmers in the world may not be very helpful. You'll probably need at least one ally facing the same temptations (food) and frustrations (family and friends). If you can't find one, join a slimming group.

Slimming used to be a women-only occupation – the last bastion of female privilege. Now even that is disappearing. More and more men slim these days – children too. But the reasons why men and women slim are different. In general, women are far more motivated by fashion and appearances than by health con-siderations. Men are more likely to re-spond to the doctor's voice telling them that their health will suffer if they don't do something about getting rid of their paunches. But even men – well, some of them – are fashion conscious. Overweight children at a very early age are made to feel different and outsiders if they are much fatter than their friends. They should be given all the help they need to lose weight, slowly and sensibly.

Who needs to slim?

The short answer is 'anyone who is too fat'!

There's no doubt that being much fatter than you should be makes it more likely that you'll get one or more of several weight-associated diseases. The disorders which are associated with overweight are well known – middle age diabetes, coro-nary heart disease, painful arthritis, hiatus hernia and high blood pressure. Very heavy people also have more ac-cidents than thin, light ones.

Being too fat, on its own, doesn't always cause these disorders, but it can make it easier for things that do cause the condition to be effective. For example, no matter what your weight, you may have a family tendency to heart disease. If you smoke you are more likely to actually have a heart attack, and being too fat as well may be the last straw.

Losing weight can reduce the risk of getting many of the diseases we've men-tioned. It can cure the symptoms of middle age diabetes and greatly ease the pain of arthritis in the hips and legs.

But being overweight also has an effect on a person's attitude to life, and his general wellbeing. Not many people feel they look their best when they are over-weight. Indeed, a recent survey showed that the majority of overweight people knew they were too fat, and many wanted

to slim. For most people slimming is worth the effort, in terms of improved health and looks. But there are a few people for whom the effort involved in losing weight is simply not worth it.

If someone has reached the age of seventy years and has been overweight for fifty of them, there is not much benefit or point in changing eating habits to lose weight.

This argument, however, is a retrospective one, and not much use to someone who is twenty years old now. No-one knows until he's reached seventy that being overweight isn't going to have much detrimental effect! So for most people under the age of about sixty slimming is worth it. Most people can lose weight successfully and still enjoy their food. But for some it really does involve considerable sacrifices. For them it may well be better to slim a little, and to settle for being a bit over ideal weight, and to enjoy life at the same time. There's no point in a long, miserable life! But this doesn't apply to the majority of people.

How many succeed in losing weight?
Fewer than five per cent of the people who start slimming lose weight and stay at their ideal weight for at least five years, give or take a kilo or two. That sounds pretty depressing, but if we know why people have failed in the past, there is a good chance you can learn from their mistakes and be successful yourself.

Quite a number of people who start to slim are not serious about it, they don't really want to be slim. Given the choice between a chocolate biscuit and keeping to a slimming diet, they would rather eat the biscuit – and another. There's no doubt that slimming does take effort, thought and willpower. Unless you really want to lose weight, you're wasting your time starting a slimming diet.

Secondly, slimming takes time. It doesn't happen overnight. So the kind of eating plan you choose must be interesting enough to allow you to keep to it for many months, even years. And thirdly it has to be flexible enough to accommodate dinner parties, entertaining and being entertained.

How to succeed
The three golden rules of success are – be determined, realise it will take time and choose an interesting diet you want to keep to. Thousands of 'slimming' diets have been published, but many of them are so rigid you couldn't keep to them for more than a week and still lead a normal, sociable life. And boredom is the reason most often given for not sticking to the slimming plan. It is precisely to rule out monotony that this book has been prepared. The recipes are suitable for the whole family, for friends and special dinner guests. You'll want to go on using them, and losing weight until you reach your goal, and after.

Ideal weight
Almost the first question every slimmer asks is – how much should I weigh? Frankly it's almost impossible to give any general sort of answer. Since ideal weight for any given height varies so much, many of the tables produced are not very useful for individuals. Even the tables which give ideal weights for different bone structures are not all that precise. But they can be a rough guide (see Table 1, p. 132).

By far the best policy is to look in the mirror, be honest and realise that you have some weight to lose. Start slimming and from week to week weigh yourself to see if you are making progress. As the weeks go by a critical reappraisal of your shape in the mirror will tell you whether you have lost enough weight. When the reflection pleases you, stop slimming and start eating a little more to maintain your ideal weight. But do remember that not everyone is meant to have vital statistics of 34, 24, 34, Be realistic and accept that you may not be one of the world's sylphs.

How long will it take?

Crash diets claim you can lose 2.5 kg (5 lb) in three days. Maybe, but much of that is water and will be replaced very quickly. It's fat you are trying to lose and this book is not about crash diets. A healthy slimming diet should enable most adults to lose an average of 0.5 to 1.5 kg (1 to 3 lb) per week. At the beginning of any slimming diet you are likely to lose weight faster than you do towards the end. The human body is not an entirely predictable machine and although you may be eating precisely the same number of calories week in and week out, weight loss can be variable. Some weeks you may not lose anything at all.

Of course, if you know you've been eating twice your set calorie allowance you have only yourself to blame. But as long as you are keeping to the calorie allowance, no matter what the scales say, you will be losing body fat. The fluctuations in weight loss from week to week are often due to changes in the amount of water in the body. There is no need for you to drink less water, tea or coffee, indeed you should not try to restrict fluid intake as this can be dangerous in the long term. Your body will automatically make the fluid adjustments for you.

For children the weight loss to aim at is from 0 to 1 kg (0 to 2 lb) a week. That may sound silly, but a normal weight child who is actively growing should be using a lot of energy in upward growth. And he should gain weight. An overweight child may well grow in height, stay the same weight and so actually be losing body fat. It is very important that children develop a healthy attitude to slimming. It is possible that some will become so obsessed with their weight that they refuse all food completely. Once this condition takes hold it is difficult to cure. So the rule with children is either to change their diets without them knowing much about it, or to give encouragement but play down the actual overweight bit. Treat the exercise in a matter of fact way, and encourage them to take vigorous exercise and to play out of doors as much as possible.

What sort of slimming plan?

You've probably heard of the low carbohydrate diet, the low fat diet, the grapefruit diet and the meal replacement diet – and a few dozen more. No matter what the diet may be called, if it results in you eating less energy than you need, you'll lose weight. But it's not 100 per cent certain that all the so-called slimming diets on the market will actually cut total energy intake.

Your body fat is basically a store of energy (measured in calories). The energy is part of the fat molecules. The energy in food and drink is contained within the protein, fat, starch, sugar and alcohol. (There is no energy in water, minerals or vitamins). If you eat more energy than you use up each day you'll *probably* store the excess as body fat. For most people the excess protein, fat, starch, sugar and alcohol you eat is all converted into body fat. So the energy changes from one form – in food – to another – your fat.

The converse of storing energy is using it during slimming when you eat too little energy. Your body demands that it has enough energy to live and be active and if you don't eat enough, body fat is broken down to release its energy and you lose weight.

The one foolproof, sure-to-succeed way

to lose weight is to calculate the amount of energy you now eat each day and to make sure you eat less than that. In other words you count calories. It doesn't matter whether the calories are in protein, fat, sugar, starch or alcohol. A calorie is a calorie.

This may be surprising to the devotees of the low carbohydrate diet. They may well have been led to believe that if all they have to do to lose weight is to cut down on carbohydrate (starch and sugar) this alone must have been responsible for their excess weight in the first place. That is not true.

But the diet may work, if by eating less carbohydrate you also eat fewer calories, but if you eat too much of the no-carbohydrate foods like cheese and meat, you won't cut calories.

A similar argument applies to the low fat diet. You may lose weight, and you may not. But there is no doubt that the calorie counted diet works for almost everyone in good health – providing you don't cheat.

How many calories a day?
On average, women need about 2100 Calories a day to stay the same weight. Some need as few as 1500, others as many as 3000 Calories. The average for men is about 2800 Calories with a range of about 2200 to 3500 depending on activity and individual body chemistry (metabolism).

As long as you eat fewer calories than you, personally, need, you'll lose weight. Unfortunately there's no way of knowing whether you normally need a few or a lot of calories to maintain weight except by you counting. But taking the lowest need of about 1500 Calories, even these women will lose weight by eating 1200 or 1000 Calories a day. And if women who have high normal energy needs eat 1200 or 1000 Calories a day they will lose weight faster than the average. If you are one of the lucky people who has relatively high energy needs, you'll be able to slim on 1500 Calories a day. It really is a matter of finding out for yourself just how many calories suit you.

In practice most women will lose weight successfully by eating about 1200 Calories a day. For men and most children the figure is about 1500 Calories. Up to a point, the lower your energy intake, the more your own fat has to supply energy to make up the deficit and the faster you lose weight. *BUT* in practice it has been shown that if you eat fewer than about 800 Calories a day you begin to use a large amount of body protein (muscle) to supply the energy you need. This clearly is not the idea at all. You are trying to lose fat. So about 800 is the absolute minimum energy intake anyone should have. Starvation is definitely out, unless it is undertaken at the direction of a doctor, usually in hospital.

The value of exercise
There is a great deal to be said for most of us taking more exercise to promote better all round health. In that context every little helps. The trouble with exercise aimed at losing weight is that it needs to be taken frequently to do any good. An hour a week on the tennis court or rugby pitch isn't going to use up much more than 500 Calories. Averaged over the week that is about 70 Calories a day – the equivalent of one slice of bread (no butter).

For most of us, it would be difficult to fit in enough activity to make any impact on body weight. So food restriction must be the main weapon to attack body fat. But for the general health of heart and lungs any extra activity you can do will be a benefit.

What to eat
For someone who needs 2200 Calories a

day to maintain weight, cutting intake to 1100 Calories means, very simply, eating half as much food. Unfortunately it isn't quite that straightforward. If you eat half your normal amount of food, but keep the types of foods the same, it follows that you halve, not only the calories but also the protein, vitamins and minerals. This would only be satisfactory if your normal food gave you twice as much of all these nutrients as you actually need. It is most unlikely that this is so. Therefore an indiscriminate halving of food intake is not going to give you enough of the many nutrients you need to keep healthy.

Even this wouldn't matter so much if your slimming plan was a short sharp one. You could use your body stores of nutrients to tide you over. But your diet isn't going to be a seven day wonder. Seven months or even years would be nearer the mark because you're going to use the same basic plan to stay slim, and no one has enough body stores of nutrients to last that long.

Clearly then your slimming diet has to pack in more nutrients per 100 Calories than ordinary, weight-maintaining eating. You need to know something (not a lot) about the nutrients in different foods relative to their calorie values. Then you can cut calories without going short of vitamins and minerals.

The balanced diet
Very few foods provide only one nutrient.

Some contain two or three while others have a dozen or so. Sugar, lard, cooking oils provide one nutrient each. Sugar is almost solid carbohydrate and lard and cooking oils are 100 per cent fat. In both cases that means they give you energy (calories) but no proteins, vitamins or minerals. On purely nutritional grounds they could well be reduced dramatically in the diet, and you'd cut a lot of energy.

The more nutritious foods are those which provide proteins and/or vitamins and/or minerals as well as energy. Remember that energy comes from fats, carbohydrates, alcohol and proteins. There are dozens of nutrients you need to eat in food and drink. No single food contains them all in the proportions you need and the easiest way of making sure you eat them all is to eat many different kinds of foods regularly. Table 2 (see page 137) shows you the main nutrients in some foods. Most foods make a contribution to mineral intake. Energy (measured in calories) isn't mentioned in this table because it isn't a nutrient. It is part of protein, fat, carbohydrate and alcohol. Almost all foods except sweets, sugar and pure fats provide nutrients other than the energy giving ones.

Energy values of foods
But even within these nutritious foods, some provide more energy than others. In general, foods with a high fat content – butter, double cream, cheese, most nuts,

chocolate, pastry – have high energy values (see Table 3, page 137). And foods with very little water usually contain more calories than those with a lot of water (see Table 3, page 137). Of course, these are general rules and it is possible to have a food like milk which has a lot of water but a lot of fat too, so it is rather rich in calories.

A detailed list of foods and their calorie contents is given at the back of this book (see pages 138-142). Remember that it's important to notice the amount of food the energy figures refer to.

Cooking food

Very often people see that foods like white fish and fish cakes are low in calories and they completely forget about cooking. Yet the method used can sometimes have a dramatic effect on the number of calories you actually eat. Some foods absorb a great deal of fat, others will lose fat. In general, foods with a fair proportion of bread or potato, or those with a crumb coating absorb fat whether they're fried or brushed liberally with fat before being grilled. So brush very sparingly with oil before grilling.

Meats, on the other hand, will almost always lose fat whether they are fried or grilled. But you can see how important the method of cooking is for some foods from the following figures:

1 fish cake, grilled without fat
  60 Calories
1 fish cake shallow fat fried
  160 Calories
2 oz (50 g) onion raw   *10 Calories*
2 oz (50 g) onion, fried   *170 Calories*
2 oz (50 g) mushrooms, raw
  10 Calories
2 oz (50 g) mushrooms, fried
  100 Calories

Practical nutrition

It's all very well saying that fats and sugars contain calories and not many nutrients like vitamins and minerals so they can well be cut right down in a slimming diet. In practice though, these are two of the components which help to make foods pleasant to eat. A diet with very little fat is decidedly unpleasant – dry bread, potatoes without butter or margarine, no Cheddar-type cheese, cream or fried foods. It must be said that, with a bit of effort, many people can get used to eating habits they thought they'd never tolerate. Equally, there is no point in going through agony to eat some things you really hate. Even a slimming diet has room for some choco-late, some cake, some fried food, as long as you know the calorie values of the foods and overall your diet is a well balanced one. The emphasis should be on changing the balance of foods you eat rather than eliminating some foods for all time.

There are now many foods on the market which are designed especially for slimmers to help them cut calories and still enjoy food. Some of these are very useful, others are a complete waste of money. Among the more useful foods are those which give sweetness without calories. Low calorie jams and sugar substitutes for use in tea and coffee, and in cooking. Low calorie soft drinks can help too. Equally useful are foods with a reduced fat content: skimmed milk and skimmed milk pow-der, low calorie salad dressings, low fat spreads and some of the low calorie soups.

Less useful, or downright useless to the slimmer are jams and chocolates which are designed for diabetics and contain sorbitol. Sorbitol is a sweetener which is absorbed into the body much more slowly than sugar and is therefore very suitable for some diabetics who are not overweight. But sorbitol has the same number of calories as sugar and foods containing this sweetener usually have similar calorie values to 'ordinary' equivalent foods.

They're fine for normal weight diabetics, but they won't help you cut calories.

Many low carbohydrate beers contain the same number of calories as the ordinary equivalents. High protein breakfast cereals and crispbreads in which protein replaces some of the starch have precisely the same number of calories as ordinary equivalents. Since you are most unlikely to be short of protein anyway, you don't need more.

Meal substitutes designed for slimmers are many and varied. Some are small portions of ordinary food, often with a sprinkling of vitamins and minerals. Some, but not all, are flavoured milk or skimmed milk again with a few extra vitamins and minerals. The latter in particular are not a very good idea in the long term if what you really want is to change your diet permanently so that you not only lose weight but also keep slim. Certainly these products will help you lose weight if you follow the instructions in the packets, but they won't help you learn what was wrong with your eating habits in the first place. As soon as you 'come off the diet' you'll go back to the old habits and probably put back some or all of the weight you lost.

So you have to be discriminating about the foods sold specifically for slimmers. Find out how many calories they are going to give you and whether they are saving calories on 'normal' equivalents. If they are, and you like the taste, use them. But don't imagine that everything which is labelled for slimmers, is necessarily calorie reduced.

The value of fibre

In the last few years dietary fibre (the new name for roughage) has been launched on the world as the wonder food component. Many claims have been made for its health-giving, disease-preventing proper-

ties and fibre rich foods are coming on to the market at a rapid rate.

Among the benefits claimed for fibre is that if you eat enough of it you'll find slimming easier. Dietary fibre is certainly useful in treating constipation, a condition which seems to affect the slimming section of society even more than the rest. From that point of view additional fibre in the form of fruits, vegetables, nuts and wholegrain cereals will undoubtedly be valuable to many people.

Whether fibre also helps to make slimming easier is unknown. However slimmers ought to be eating quite a lot of it anyway because fruits and vegetables are filling and low in calories and ought to feature largely in the slimming diet.

What seems certain is that the bran tablets on the market which are aimed to fill you up before you eat a meal are probably not effective in doing that. They don't contain enough bran to swell sufficiently. They may work psychologically, and the slimming eating plan issued with them will certainly help you lose weight because it restricts the amount of energy you eat.

Other appetite controlling cubes are based on sugar/glucose with a few vitamins. You might as well eat an ordinary toffee. It won't have any of the vitamins, but you shouldn't need them if you are eating a varied diet.

So by now it should be obvious that there's no real substitute for will power and knowing what you're doing in the slimming game. By and large everyday foods with some of the specially prepared foods for slimmers should form the basis of meals.

How many meals a day?

Almost all 'sensible' slimming advice suggests that breakfast is a must. You may never have eaten breakfast in your life, you may be nauseated by the thought of food before noon but never mind – now that you're slimming you must eat breakfast, they say. One theory is that breakfast stops you feeling hungry until lunch time and so stops you being tempted to eat chocolate bars, biscuits and buns in the middle of the morning. For some people this is exactly what happens in practice. But for others it just doesn't work. For them not only is food in the morning repulsive, but it also makes them feel that now they've started eating they might as well go on for the rest of the day; and they eat and eat. Psychological it may be, but for some adults it is much better not to eat breakfast if they don't want it.

But for children it is different. Their last meal in the evening is usually quite early and there may be a long gap between that meal and the next if they don't eat something in the morning. Cereal and/or toast is all that's needed.

In practice it doesn't make much difference to weight loss whether you eat one or two meals day. But there could be real disadvantages in eating many times a day. The most obvious one is that it is much easier to lose track of what you've eaten and to underestimate the total number of calories you actually do eat in the day.

There are other advantages in eating meals as opposed to snacks. The kinds of foods which we eat as meals are different from those we eat as between-meal snacks. Admittedly some quick and easy-to-prepare snacks are nutritious, but many aren't. The kinds of foods you can eat without a knife and fork, without even a plate, tend to be rich in sugars and fats – chocolate bars, biscuits, cake and crisps. A lot of calories and not too many nutrients. Just a small bar of chocolate, a small packet of crisps and a few peanuts add up to at least 600 Calories.

Compare that with a good plate of lean meat (75 g/3 oz) or fish, green beans, carrots and broccoli and a medium potato, followed by a piece of fresh fruit – just 500 Calories at the most if you can find a dinner plate large enough to take that much. A good general rule is that if you can eat a food with a knife and fork, and it fits into the conventional concept of a 'proper' meal, it is likely to be better for a slimmer than most of the snacks you could substitute. There are, of course, some foods which you shouldn't eat too often even though they could be eaten with a knife and fork – pastry on meat and fruit pies, exotic cream puddings and large portions of cheese, salads smothered with oily dressings and lots of fried food.

A good policy for most slimmers is not to eat unless you are sitting at a dinner table and you can eat the food with a knife and fork. The exception is lunch in the office. But even here, if you think about it you can prepare soups and salads and take them with you.

Above all, don't eat while you're walking along the street, sitting in a train or the cinema or pushing the vacuum cleaner around the house.

Shopping

As far as home eating is concerned, it's not that difficult to control the situation. The real determinant of what you eat is what you buy. So the critical activity is shopping.

Never shop on an empty stomach because you'll be tempted to buy something to eat immediately and it's likely to be a high calorie food. Always make a list of foods you want, foods you know you can use in calorie controlled meals through the week. And don't be tempted to buy biscuits and crisps and chocolates. Once they're in the house, there's a fair chance you'll eat them. Why tempt yourself? And don't imagine you're depriving the other members of the family, they will benefit from the new eating plan even if they complain for the first few days.

If you are the only person in the house who is trying to lose weight, you still don't have to prepare two sets of meals, for you and them. Your meals can be adapted for the non-slimmers by giving them more potato or bread, by giving them all the pastry on a pie and by making puddings for them while you eat fresh fruit.

Entertaining and being entertained

Even when you invite people to dinner, there's no reason why you should feel obliged to get through a packet of butter and a pint of double cream. There are plenty of recipes in this book you can use to impress your friends with your culinary skills and still have the satisfaction of knowing that you've kept to your calorie allowance. Even restaurant eating shouldn't be a problem. Going to someone else's home may well be a different matter. In general it's far better not to tell anyone, except perhaps your nearest and dearest that you're 'on a diet'. That way you avoid so-called friends trying to tempt you with foods you know you shouldn't be eating, you avoid making real friends feel embarrased that they may give you something which will ruin three months of hard work on your part (which is impossible of course), and most important of all you avoid being a slimming bore.

It is important to lose weight, it isn't all that easy, and it does take time. You are to be congratulated when you've won. But please make it a personal battle between you and your consuming passion and don't involve everyone around you. Slimming may take over your life, but don't imagine that all the other inhabitants of your town are just as interested.

So when you know you're going to someone's home for a meal, plan ahead, eat less the day before. Then you and everyone else can eat what has been prepared and enjoy it.

Alcohol

On the subject of parties and entertaining, please don't forget alcohol. It is amazing how many people are quite prepared to count the calories in the solid foods they eat, but for some reason they forget about the calories in liquids. Water has none, but the moment you dissolve sugar or alcohol in it things change. And a calorie is a calorie whether it's in a solid or a liquid. Alcoholic drinks, especially those you drink by the pint or half pint, soon pile on the calories. It is better to keep to spirits well diluted with soda or low-calorie mixers. Or mix dry white wine with soda. Best of all take the low-calorie mixer on its own.

Going off the straight and narrow

No matter how well you plan ahead and how strong your will power, there will be days when things go wrong. You feel depressed – and eat. You go out unexpectedly to see a friend and eat her lovingly prepared food. Days like this will happen, but don't let them get you down. It's very easy for one bad day to make you think you've blown your diet for ever. But if you think for a minute you'll realise this can't be true. Forget it and start again on the proper slimming plan the next day. And resist the temptation to get the bathroom scales out to see the damage.

With the help of the charts in the back of this book, and the recipes you're ready to start slimming, to change your eating habits for the rest of your life.

● First buy yourself a small notebook to keep a record of all the food and drink you take each day. It's the only way to be sure you don't cheat and it's not that much of an effort after the first few days.

● Weigh yourself on day 1 and write the weight down. Thereafter, weigh yourself once or twice a week at the same time of day.

● In deciding what to eat, remember to eat as many different foods as possible. White fish, poultry, fruits and vegetables are especially low in calories. Lean meats, eggs, low fat cheeses, skimmed milk and natural yogurt are nutritious and quite modest in energy while foods like hard cheeses, butter and margarine, pastry, chocolate, nuts and alcoholic drinks should be taken infrequently. Try to include some bread, both white and wholemeal in the diet and eat wholewheat pasta occasionally.

● Do allow yourself a 'treat' from time to time – which doesn't mean at every meal. Once a week allowing yourself your favourite, high calorie food, in small amounts won't do any harm. But if you are one of those people who can't stop eating chocolates until the whole box is gone, it's better not to buy any and not to start eating them.

● Once you've slimmed to your ideal weight, add about 100 Calories a day for a week and see what happens to your weight. That way you can find your maintenance calorie requirement and stay within 1 kg (2 lb) of your target weight for ever!

Guide to calorie counts

All the recipes in this book include a calorie count for both metric and Imperial quantities. This can be found at the top of each recipe and refers to the total recipe. Where metric and Imperial quantities differ only a little this figure is the same. Only when the quantities differ appreciably have both figures been calculated separately.

Alongside this total recipe calorie count is another figure, in brackets, this refers to the individual portion calorie count of the recipe. Remember to adjust this figure if you eat either more or less than the recommended serving.

Good luck.

17

Breakfasts

Even if you don't eat breakfast, don't pass by these recipes on the assumption they're not for you. Non-breakfast eaters will find many of these recipes suitable for many meal occasions not just breakfast. Try Kippered Eggs or Cottage Eggs as starters to main meals.

The drinks make ideal quick meals when you've absolutely no time – and they are so much better for you and your diet than chocolate biscuits or crisps.

Swiss Toasts and Ocean Toasties make good savoury endings to formal meals if you want a change from traditional sweet puddings.

If you do like eating breakfast remember to use Sprinkle Sweet (6 Calories per tablespoon) on breakfast cereals. You'll find something in the breakfast recipes to ring the changes on the ever popular cereals, toast and boiled egg. It's wise to eat only about 200 to 250 Calories at breakfast time – so that you have a good reserve for the rest of the day. You never know whether you'll be invited out to lunch or dinner. Or maybe you'll have one of those days when food is the only consolation. Anyway, you know you have enough calories left still to keep to your allowance.

If you want to stay with your trusted egg and toast remember the calories:

1 slice ordinary bread **90 Calories**	spread with butter **150 Calories**
1 slice Slimcea **35 Calories**	spread with Outline **70 Calories**
1 boiled egg **90 Calories**	
1 portion of most breakfast cereals about **100 Calories**	
150 ml/¼ pint milk **100 Calories**	
150 ml/¼ pint Marvel **50 Calories**	
1 teaspoon sugar **20 Calories**	
1 Hermesetas Tablet **0 Calories**	
1 teaspoon Hermesetas Sprinkle Sweet **2 Calories**	
1 teaspoon Hermesetas Liquid Sweetener **3.8 Calories**	

Slimmers' Muesli (see page 21); Kippered Eggs (see page 22)

Slimmers' Muesli

See photograph on page 19
Serves 4

Metric		Imperial
600 (150)	CALORIES	**600 (150)**
65 g	**porridge oats**	2½ oz
½ teaspoon	**Hermesetas Liquid Sweetener**	½ teaspoon
250 ml	**made-up Marvel**	8 fl oz
2	**dessert apples**	2
25 g	**sultanas or raisins**	1 oz
15 g	**walnuts**	½ oz

Turn the oats into a large bowl. Mix the Hermesetas and Marvel together. Coarsely grate the apples and mix into the oats with the sultanas or raisins. Chop the walnuts coarsely and stir into the oat, apple and fruit mixture. Pour the sweetened Marvel into the bowl and allow to soak for 1 hour before serving if liked.

Breakfast Crunch

Serves 6

Metric		Imperial
720 (120)	CALORIES	**720 (120)**
50 g	**wheat flakes**	2 oz
25 g	**sultanas**	1 oz
25 g	**demerara sugar**	1 oz
25 g	**currants**	1 oz
15 g	**walnuts, chopped**	½ oz
25 g	**dried apricots, chopped**	1 oz
15 g	**dried apple, chopped**	½ oz
450 ml	**Marvel Yogurt (see page 98)**	¾ pint

Mix all the dry ingredients together. Divide the yogurt between six bowls and serve the crunch on top.

Morning Rise (see page 24); Orange Yogurt Drink (see page 25); Mocha Breakfast Drink (see page 25)

Kippered Eggs

See photograph on page 19
Serves 4

Metric		Imperial
840 (210)	CALORIES	**840 (210)**
2 (weighing about 175 g each)	**kippers**	2 (weighing about 6 oz each)
2	**eggs**	2
25 g	**Outline**	1 oz
2 tablespoons	**made-up Marvel**	2 tablespoons
	salt and pepper	
4	**slices Slimcea**	4

Cook the kippers in a little water until tender, about 5 minutes. Drain well and flake the flesh, removing any bones. Beat the eggs and add the Outline, Marvel and seasoning to taste. Pour into a saucepan and stir in the flaked kipper flesh. Cook over a low heat, stirring continuously until the egg starts to set, about 3-5 minutes. Meanwhile lightly toast the Slimcea and serve the egg mixture on the toast.

Ocean Toasties

Serves 4

Metric		Imperial
860 (215)	CALORIES	**860 (215)**
8	**slices Slimcea**	8
25 g	**Outline**	1 oz
1 (227-g) can	**pilchards in tomato sauce**	1 (8-oz) can
	salt and pepper	
2	**eggs**	2
2 tablespoons	**made-up Marvel**	2 tablespoons
	knob of Outline	
	Garnish	
	chopped parsley	

Toast the Slimcea and spread with the Outline. Place the pilchards and their sauce in a bowl. Season lightly and mash thoroughly. Divide the pilchards between the toast and spread over the top. Beat the eggs with the Marvel and a little seasoning. Place the toast and the pilchards under a hot grill to heat through. Meanwhile melt the knob of Outline in a small saucepan, add the egg mixture and cook over a low heat, stirring continuously until the egg starts to set, about 2-3 minutes. Arrange a little scrambled egg on the pilchards, garnish with chopped parsley and serve immediately.

Swiss Toasts

Serves 4

Metric		Imperial
960 (240)	CALORIES	**960 (240)**
4	slices Slimcea	4
25 g	**Outline**	1 oz
	a little prepared mustard	
4 slices	**lean ham**	4 slices
4 slices	**Cheddar cheese**	4 slices
2	**tomatoes**	2
	Garnish	
	few sprigs parsley	

Toast the Slimcea on one side only. Spread the uncooked sides with Outline and a little mustard. Arrange, mustard side up, on a baking tray and cover with a slice of lean ham and cheese. Cook in a moderate oven (180°C, 350°F, Gas Mark 4) for about 5 minutes or until the cheese melts. Cut the tomatoes into quarters and place two wedges on each piece of toast. Return to the oven until the tomato has heated through, about 5 minutes. Garnish with a sprig of parsley and top with more mustard if liked.

Alternatively, the cheese may be melted under a moderate grill, the tomato added and heated slowly under the grill before serving as above.

Cottage Eggs

Serves 4

Metric		Imperial
740 (185)	CALORIES	**740 (185)**
4	**eggs**	4
	salt and pepper	
6 tablespoons	**made–up Marvel**	6 tablespoons
	knob of Outline	
225 g	**cottage cheese**	8 oz
4	**slices brown Slimcea**	4

Beat the eggs with seasoning to taste in a bowl. Beat in the Marvel until the mixture is frothy. Melt the Outline in a saucepan, add the egg mixture and cook over a low heat until the egg starts to set, about 3 minutes. Quickly stir in the cottage cheese and heat through. Meanwhile toast the Slimcea, cut the slices in half and serve with the eggs.

Breakfast Omelettes

Serves 4

Metric		Imperial
1160 (290)	CALORIES	**1160 (290)**
	Omelettes	
8	**eggs**	8
	salt and pepper	
25 g	**Outline**	1 oz
	Filling	
350 g	**cooked smoked haddock**	12 oz
1 tablespoon	**chopped parsley**	1 tablespoon
1 tablespoon	**chopped chives (optional)**	1 tablespoon

First prepare the omelette filling. Remove any skin and bones from the fish and break it down into flakes. Mix with the herbs and season with a little pepper.

Prepare the omelettes by whisking 2 eggs with seasoning to taste and 1 teaspoon of cold water. Melt a quarter of the Outline in a non-stick omelette pan over a high heat and pour in the egg mixture. Cook quickly, lifting the sides of the omelette gently to allow any uncooked egg to run on to the pan. When the egg is lightly set, spoon in a quarter of the filling and fold the omelette in half. Slide on to a serving plate. Repeat the process to make four omelettes.

Morning Rise

See photograph on page 20
Serves 2

Metric		Imperial
420 (210)	CALORIES	**420 (210)**
6	**cooked prunes, stones removed**	6
3 heaped tablespoons	**dry Marvel**	3 heaped tablespoons
450 ml	**unsweetened orange juice**	$\frac{3}{4}$ pint
	Decoration	
	slices of orange (optional)	

Turn all the ingredients except the orange slices into a liquidiser and blend until smooth. Chill and serve in glasses decorated with orange slices if liked.

Mocha Breakfast Drink

See photograph on page 20
Serves 1

Metric		Imperial
80	CALORIES	**80**
200 ml	**made-up Marvel**	$\frac{1}{3}$ pint
2 teaspoons	**cocoa powder**	2 teaspoons
1 teaspoon	**instant coffee**	1 teaspoon
	few drops Hermesetas Liquid Sweetener	
	pinch of ground cinnamon (optional)	

Put all the ingredients except the ground cinnamon into a saucepan and whisk until almost boiling. Pour into a mug and sprinkle the top with cinnamon if liked.

Orange Yogurt Drink

See photograph on page 20
Serves 1

Metric		Imperial
95	CALORIES	**95**
150 ml	**Marvel Yogurt (see page 98)**	$\frac{1}{4}$ pint
$\frac{1}{2}$ teaspoon	**grated orange rind**	$\frac{1}{2}$ teaspoon
4 tablespoons	**unsweetened orange juice**	4 tablespoons
$\frac{1}{4}-\frac{1}{2}$ teaspoon	**Hermesetas Liquid Sweetener**	$\frac{1}{4}-\frac{1}{2}$ teaspoon
	Decoration	
1	**slice of orange**	1

Stir the yogurt, orange rind and juice together. Add Hermesetas to taste. When well mixed pour into a glass and chill. Serve decorated with a slice of orange.

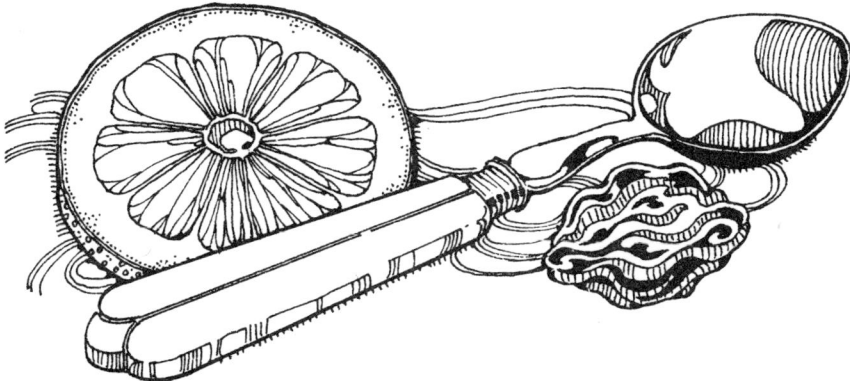

——— *Starters and soups* ———

Why don't the British eat more soup? People in almost every other European country consider soup an important part of a meal, or even a meal by itself. In this country, soup is much underrated. Perhaps we are too conscious of the difficulty of eating delicately!

Just think of the varieties of soup – meat, fish, vegetable, hot or cold, thick or thin. Almost all soups freeze well, so one morning's concentrated soup-making should see you through the month. If you want to save freezer space, use only half the amount of stock or water suggested in the recipe. Do remember to make the volume up when you're reheating the soup.

Soups like Bortsh and Golden Vegetable look very attractive, as well as tasting good. Cold soups like Cucumber and Mint can be prepared well in advance and make a refreshing start to a summer's meal.

The calorie counts of some ready-prepared soups are high, but the recipes in this section give you as few as 40 Calories a portion. All soups are filling because they contain so much water and some, like Chicken Liver Soup are very nourishing. With some Slimcea bread they can make a good snack meal at home or in the office. (Take soup to work in a wide-neck Thermos flask).

Other starters are included here. Some are very low in calories – California Prawn Cocktail and Mushroom Cream are eminently suitable to precede heavy main courses. More substantial starters like Turkey Pots and Fish Mousse are good before lighter, salad-based meals.

Fish Mousse

Serves 4

Metric		Imperial
580 (145)	CALORIES	**580 (145)**
175 g	cooked fresh salmon or	6 oz
1 (213-g) can	canned salmon	1 (7½-oz) can
½	cucumber, peeled	½
150 ml	All-in-one Coating Sauce (see page 111)	¼ pint
15 g	powdered gelatine	½ oz
4 tablespoons	Slimmers' Mayonnaise (see page 78)	4 tablespoons
	salt and pepper	
1	egg white	1
	Garnish	
4	slices of lemon	4

Remove the skin from the salmon and flake. If using canned salmon, reserve the juices; if cooking fresh salmon, reserve the stock.

Halve the cucumber lengthways and scoop out the seeds. Dice the flesh and place in a saucepan with the reserved liquid from the can or 4 tablespoons of fish stock. Bring to the boil and simmer for 5 minutes to partially cook the cucumber. Liquidise the salmon with the cucumber, its cooking liquid and the coating sauce until smooth. Dissolve the gelatine in 2 tablespoons of water or fish liquid in a basin over hot water.

Stir the Slimmers' Mayonnaise into the fish mixture and season lightly. Stir in the dissolved gelatine and leave until the mixture begins to set.

Whisk the egg white until stiff and fold into the fish mixture. Divide the mixture between four individual dishes. Chill well before serving garnished with twists of lemon.

Californian Prawn Cocktail

See photograph on page 29
Serves 4

Metric		Imperial
200 (50)	CALORIES	**200 (50)**
4	**small lemons**	4
2 tablespoons	**Marvel Yogurt (see page 98)**	2 tablespoons
	few drops Tabasco sauce	
$\frac{1}{4}$ teaspoon	**Hermesetas Liquid Sweetener**	$\frac{1}{4}$ teaspoon
	salt and pepper	
100 g	**peeled prawns**	4 oz
$\frac{1}{2}$	**cucumber, peeled and diced**	$\frac{1}{2}$
1 tablespoon	**capers, chopped**	1 tablespoon
1 tablespoon	**chopped parsley or chives**	1 tablespoon
	Garnish	
4	**sprigs parsley**	4

Cut the tops off the lemons and scoop out the flesh. Squeeze the juice from the lemon pulp. Mix together the yogurt, Tabasco, Hermesetas and 2 tablespoons of the lemon juice. Season to taste then add the prawns, cucumber, capers and parsley or chives to the dressing and toss well. Spoon the mixture into the lemon shells and chill. Garnish each lemon with a sprig of parsley.

Mushroom Cream

See photograph on page 134
Serves 4

Metric		Imperial
180 (45)	CALORIES	**180 (45)**
225 g	**button mushrooms, sliced**	8 oz
150 ml	**Marvel Yogurt (see page 98)**	$\frac{1}{4}$ pint
2 tablespoons	**Slimmers' Mayonnaise (see page 78)**	2 tablespoons
2 tablespoons	**tomato purée**	2 tablespoons
	few drops Worcestershire sauce	
1 tablespoon	**lemon juice**	1 tablespoon
	salt and pepper	
	Garnish	
4	**lettuce leaves**	4
	paprika	
4	**slices of lemon**	4

Put the mushrooms in a bowl, cover with boiling water and leave to stand for 2 minutes. Drain well.

Mix the yogurt, Slimmers' Mayonnaise, tomato purée, Worcestershire sauce and lemon juice together. Stir in the mushrooms and season to taste. Chill well.

Serve the mixture on a bed of lettuce, sprinkled with paprika and garnished with twists of lemon.

Turkey Pots (see page 34); Herby Cheese Balls (see page 33); Californian Prawn Cocktail (see page 27)
Overleaf *Spicy Golden Soup (see page 36); Vegetable Bortsch (see page 35); Chicken Liver Soup (see page 34); Golden Vegetable Soup (see page 36); Herb Bread (see page 117)*

Herby Cheese Balls

See photograph on page 29
Serves 6–8

Metric		Imperial
870 (145–110)	CALORIES	**870 (145–110)**
225 g	**cottage cheese with chives**	8 oz
2 tablespoons	**mushroom soup mix**	2 tablespoons
25 g	**dry Marvel**	1 oz
75 g	**Edam cheese**	3 oz
75 g	**White Stilton cheese**	3 oz
$\frac{1}{2}$	**small onion**	$\frac{1}{2}$
1	**stick celery**	1
$\frac{1}{2}$ teaspoon	**Worcestershire sauce**	$\frac{1}{2}$ teaspoon
	pinch of cayenne pepper	
4 tablespoons	**finely chopped parsley or celery leaves**	4 tablespoons

Beat the cottage cheese, soup mix and Marvel together thoroughly. Grate the Edam and Stilton cheese and finely chop the onion and celery. Add to the cheese mixture with the Worcestershire sauce and cayenne pepper and mix well. Chill the mixture thoroughly until firm. Divide into 16 balls of even size. Roll the balls in the chopped parsley or celery leaves, pressing the coating on well. Chill until firm. Serve with crispbread or Slimcea Melba Toast (see below) and raw vegetables.

Note: *These cheese balls are also delicious rolled in chopped nuts but do calculate the additional calories they provide.*

Slimcea Melba Toast

See photograph on page 29

Metric		Imperial
180	CALORIES	**180**
4	**slices Slimcea**	4

Lightly toast the Slimcea on both sides. Cut off the crusts and, working fairly quickly while the bread is still warm, slice horizontally through each piece of toast to give two thin slices toasted on one side only. Place the thin slices under the grill, untoasted side uppermost and toast lightly. The bread should curl to give thin, crisp pieces of toast. Serve with soups, pâtés and savoury dishes.

Cucumber and Mint Soup (see page 37); Slimcea Melba Toast (see above); Greek Lemon Soup (see page 38)

Turkey Pots

See photograph on page 29
Serves 8

Metric		Imperial
960 (120)	CALORIES	**960 (120)**
	few sprigs tarragon	
450 g	**cooked white turkey meat**	1 lb
	salt and black pepper	
2 tablespoons	**lemon juice**	2 tablespoons
50 g	**Outline**	2 oz
1	**lettuce, shredded**	1
	Garnish	
1	**large lemon**	1

Strip the leaves from the tarragon sprigs and chop them finely. Mince the turkey and add seasoning to taste, the lemon juice and chopped tarragon. Pound the meat mixture until smooth and creamy then work in the Outline.

Divide the mixture between eight individual small ramekin dishes and press down well. Chill and turn out if liked.

Make a bed of shredded lettuce on a serving dish and turn the pots out on to it. Cut the lemon into wedges and use as a garnish. Serve with Slimcea Melba Toast (see page 33).

Chicken Liver Soup

See photograph on page 30
Serves 4-6

Metric		Imperial
780 (195-130)	CALORIES	**780 (195-130)**
225 g	**chicken livers**	8 oz
1	**onion, chopped**	1
25 g	**Outline**	1 oz
1 tablespoon	**flour**	1 tablespoon
	pinch of powdered rosemary	
	salt and pepper	
300 ml	**chicken stock (made with a stock cube)**	$\frac{1}{2}$ pint
50 g	**dry Marvel**	2 oz
2 tablespoons	**medium dry sherry**	2 tablespoons
	gravy browning (optional)	
	Garnish	
	chopped parsley	

Clean the livers, removing any sinews. Mix with the chopped onion. Melt the Outline in a saucepan and sauté the liver and onion until the onion is soft. Stir in the flour, rosemary seasoning and gradually add the stock. Bring to the boil, cover and simmer for 15 minutes. Sieve or liquidise the soup and return it to a clean saucepan. Make up the Marvel with 300 ml/½ pint water, add to the soup with the sherry. A little gravy browning may be stirred into the soup if liked. Reheat without boiling.

Sprinkle with chopped parsley before serving. Crisp croûtons made from Slimcea bread go very well with this soup.

Vegetable Bortsch

See photograph on page 30
Serves 8

Metric		Imperial
360 (45)	CALORIES	**360 (45)**
1	onion	1
2	carrots	2
1	stick celery	1
1	parsnip	1
25 g	Outline	1 oz
1	medium beetroot	1
1.75 litres	chicken stock (made with 3 stock cubes)	3 pints
¼	medium white cabbage	¼
1	clove garlic, crushed	1
2	tomatoes	2
1 tablespoon	tomato purée	1 tablespoon
	salt and pepper	
1 tablespoon	chopped parsley	1 tablespoon
	Garnish	
8 tablespoons	Marvel Yogurt (see page 98)	8 tablespoons

Peel and cut the onion, carrot, celery and parsnip into matchstick strips. Melt the Outline in a saucepan and sauté the prepared vegetables for 5 minutes. Cut the beetroot into matchstick strips and add to the vegetables with the stock. Bring to the boil, cover and simmer for 25–30 minutes. Wash and shred the cabbage and add with the garlic. Simmer, uncovered, for a further 20 minutes. Peel the tomatoes, remove the seeds and chop very coarsely. Add to the soup with the tomato purée and seasoning. The flavour should be piquant, not sweet. Simmer for a further 10 minutes and add the parsley. Serve in individual bowls with a tablespoon of Marvel Yogurt swirled into each one.

Note: *This Bortsch improves if kept in a cool place overnight before serving.*

Spicy Golden Soup

See photograph on page 30
Serves 4

Metric		Imperial
460 (115)	CALORIES	**520 (130)**
75 g	dry Marvel	3 oz
900 ml	chicken stock (made with 2 stock cubes)	1½ pints
3 teaspoons	curry powder	3 teaspoons
1 tablespoon	tomato purée	1 tablespoon
1 teaspoon	ground turmeric	1 teaspoon
	salt and pepper	
1	medium onion, peeled	1
100 g	potato, peeled	4 oz
1	cooking or sharp dessert apple	1
	Garnish	
	paprika or cayenne pepper	

Mix the Marvel, stock, curry powder, tomato purée, turmeric and seasoning together. Chop the onion and potato roughly and add to the liquid. Bring to the boil, cover and simmer for about 30 minutes or until the vegetables are soft. Liquidise or sieve the soup and return it to a clean pan. Peel, core and chop the apple and add to the soup. Adjust seasoning and simmer for 5 minutes. Sprinkle with paprika or cayenne pepper.

Golden Vegetable Soup

See photograph on page 30
Serves 4

Metric		Imperial
520 (130)	CALORIES	**520 (130)**
100 g	carrot	4 oz
100 g	parsnip	4 oz
100 g	swede	4 oz
225 g	leeks	8 oz
2	sticks celery	2
25 g	Outline	1 oz
50 g	lentils	2 oz
600 ml	chicken stock (made with a stock cube)	1 pint
	salt and pepper	
	Garnish	
	chopped parsley (optional)	

Peel and dice the carrot, parsnip and swede finely. Wash and slice the leeks and chop the celery. Melt the Outline in a saucepan and fry the vegetables over a low heat for 5 minutes.

Stir in the lentils, stock and seasoning, bring to the boil, cover and simmer for 35–40 minutes. Garnish with chopped parsley before serving if used.

Cucumber and Mint Soup

See photograph on page 32
Serves 4-6

Metric		Imperial
280 (70-45)	CALORIES	280 (70-45)
1	**large cucumber**	1
1	**onion**	1
3	**sprigs mint**	3
600 ml	**chicken stock (made with a stock cube)**	1 pint
	salt and pepper	
50 g	**dry Marvel**	2 oz
1 teaspoon	**lemon juice**	1 teaspoon
	Garnish	
	few sprigs mint	

Cut a few thin slices of cucumber and reserve for garnishing. Remove half of the peel from the remaining cucumber and chop the cucumber roughly. Chop the onion and mint. Place the cucumber, onion and mint in a saucepan with the stock. Season lightly. Bring to the boil, cover and simmer for 20–30 minutes or until the onion is tender. Sieve or liquidise the soup until smooth. Allow to cool. Make the Marvel up to 300 ml/½ pint with cold water and stir into the soup. Adjust the seasoning if necessary. Add the lemon juice for sharpness just before serving. Garnish with the remaining cucumber and mint.

Note: *If fresh mint is not available, chopped chives may be used.*

Greek Lemon Soup

See photograph on page 32
Serves 4-6

Metric		Imperial
330 (82-55)	CALORIES	330 (82-55)
2	chicken stock cubes	2
1.15 litres	boiling water	2 pints
2	small lemons	2
50 g	cooked chicken meat, diced	2 oz
1	egg yolk	1
25 g	dry Marvel	1 oz
1 teaspoon	chopped parsley	1 teaspoon

Dissolve the stock cubes in the water and place in a medium saucepan. Add the juice of 1 lemon and the chicken. Bring to the boil then cool slightly. Whisk in the egg yolk, Marvel and parsley. Garnish the soup with the remaining lemon cut into thin slices. Serve hot or cold.

Slimcea Croûtons

Metric		Imperial
335	CALORIES	350
4	slices Slimcea, crusts removed	4
50 g	Outline	2 oz

Cut the Slimcea into cubes. Melt the Outline in a frying pan and add the bread cubes. Toss gently in the Outline, taking care to keep the cubes separate. Cook slowly until brown and crisp on one side then turn and brown the other side. Drain on absorbent kitchen paper and serve as a garnish for soups, casseroles and salads.

Variations:

Garlic croûtons – add 1 crushed clove of garlic to the Outline before adding the Slimcea cubes.

Herby croûtons – add 1 tablespoon chopped fresh herbs (parsley, thyme, sage, rosemary, chives) to the Outline before adding the Slimcea cubes.

Lemon croûtons – toss freshly cooked croûtons in the grated rind of 1 lemon before serving with fish dishes.

Main courses

It's sometimes difficult to ring the changes on cod, beef, pork and lamb, especially when you're restricted to 1200 Calories a day. The main course of the main meal should account for the largest proportion of your daily calories, but it is not difficult to let things get completely out of hand and finish up with a meal of 1500 Calories, or more. Remember that fat is the biggest culprit in pushing calories up, sometimes without your being aware of it.

A portion of steak and kidney – about 100 g/4 oz – could be about 250 Calories. Add a piece of shortcrust pastry and the amount rockets to 500. Fatty sauces and gravy, fat meat and fatty vegetables like chips all add unnecessary calories.

Choose white fish more often because it has almost no fat and is very low in calories – providing you cook it properly. Remove as much fat as possible from meat and don't eat the skin of poultry. Just as humans do, chickens store their fat beneath the skin.

Most of the recipes for main courses provide under 400 Calories. Those with about 200-250 Calories leave you plenty of room for potatoes or rice. Main courses with higher calorie counts should be accompanied by green vegetables and salads only.

Kidney and liver are good sources of iron and should be eaten once a week. Try Baked Liver Loaf and Gingered Kidney Casserole – they are a far cry from plain grilled liver and stewed kidneys. Chops aren't such a good buy as leaner cuts of meat for slimmers as it is difficult to remove fat. But if you like eating fat, you'll have to budget for the calories that come with it. And do remember that wine contains calories too. A normal size glass has about 100 Calories, so perhaps you'd like to substitute a pudding for a glass of wine occasionally.

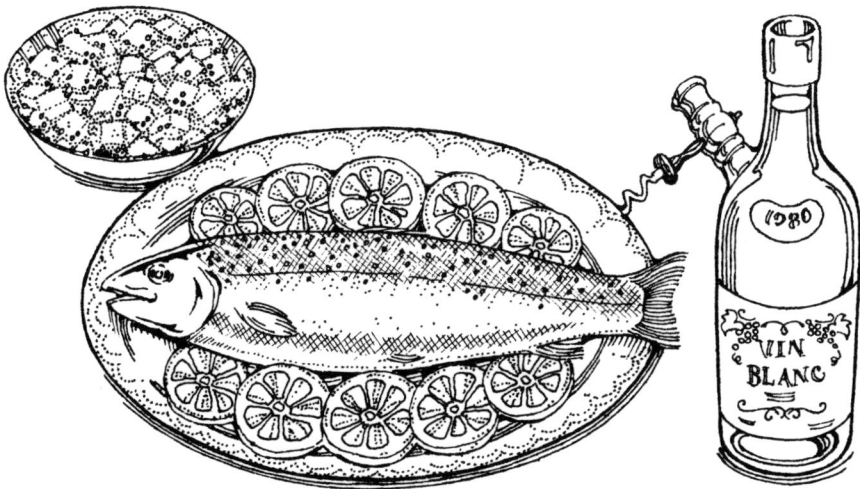

Stuffed Cod with Lemon

Serves 4

Metric		Imperial
640 (160)	CALORIES	**640 (160)**
4 (weighing about 100 g each)	**small cod steaks**	4 (weighing about 4 oz each)
	salt and pepper	
	grated rind and juice of 2 medium lemons	
6 tablespoons	**Slimcea breadcrumbs**	6 tablespoons
1 tablespoon	**chopped chives**	1 tablespoon
50 g	**Outline, melted**	2 oz
	Garnish	
1	**bunch watercress**	1
	slices of lemon	

Remove any pieces of bone from the cod. Season well and arrange in the grill pan. Mix together the lemon rind, breadcrumbs and chives with 25 g/1 oz of the Outline. Add seasoning to taste. Use this mixture to stuff the centre of each cod steak. Sprinkle the lemon juice and remaining Outline over the fish. Grill for 5 minutes on each side, turning carefully with a fish slice and basting frequently with the liquid. Serve garnished with sprigs of watercress and twists of lemon.

Crunchy Haddock Casserole

See photograph on page 49
Serves 4

Metric		Imperial
1020 (255)	CALORIES	**1080 (270)**
450 g	**tomatoes**	1 lb
25 g	**Outline**	1 oz
1	**large onion, chopped**	1
50 g	**button mushrooms, sliced**	2 oz
1 tablespoon	**chopped parsley**	1 tablespoon
	salt and pepper	
450 g	**haddock fillets, skinned**	1 lb
25 g	**Cheddar cheese, grated**	1 oz
50 g	**Outline**	2 oz
6	**slices Slimcea, crusts removed**	6
	Garnish	
	few sprigs parsley	

Peel and slice the tomatoes. Reserve a few slices for garnish and arrange the remainder in the base of a greased shallow casserole dish. Melt the 25 g/1 oz Outline in a frying pan and fry the onion until soft and transparent, add the mushrooms and cook for a few minutes. Stir in the parsley and season to taste. Arrange this mixture over the tomatoes. Cut the fish into bite-sized pieces and place on the onions and mushrooms. Sprinkle the grated cheese over the dish. Spread the Outline on the Slimcea and cut each slice in half. Arrange these with the Outline uppermost around the edge of the casserole. Bake in a moderately hot oven (190°C, 375°F, Gas Mark 5) for 40-45 minutes or until the top is golden and the fish cooked. Garnish with parsley and the reserved slices of tomato before serving.

Fish Knots

See photograph on page 49
Serves 4

Metric		Imperial
960 (240)	CALORIES	**960 (240)**
4 (100-g)	**fillets of plaice or other white fish**	4 (4-oz)
	seasoned flour for coating	
1	**egg**	1
1 tablespoon	**water**	1 tablespoon
2 tablespoons	**dry Slimcea breadcrumbs**	2 tablespoons
75 g	**Outline, melted**	3 oz
	onion salt and pepper	
½ teaspoon	**dried dill weed**	½ teaspoon
	Garnish	
	wedges of lemon	
	sprigs of watercress	

Skin the fish and cut into thin strips about 12 cm/5 inches long. Coat them with the seasoned flour and carefully tie each strip in a single knot.

Beat the egg and water together and coat the knots in the mixture. Roll each knot in the breadcrumbs.

Grease a baking tray thoroughly with some of the Outline and arrange the knots on it. Sprinkle with onion salt, pepper and dill. Drizzle the remaining Outline over the knots and cook in a moderately hot oven (200°C, 400°F, Gas Mark 6) for 15-20 minutes or until golden brown and crisp.

Serve the knots garnished with lemon wedges and watercress, accompanied by a cucumber salad.

Fish au Gratin

Serves 3

Metric		Imperial
840 (280)	CALORIES	**900 (300)**
450 g	**cod**	1 lb
300 ml	**made-up Marvel**	$\frac{1}{2}$ pint
3 tablespoons	**Slimcea breadcrumbs**	3 tablespoons
	salt and pepper	
50 g	**cheese, grated**	2 oz
1 teaspoon	**prepared mustard**	1 teaspoon

Simmer the fish in the Marvel in a skillet or deep frying pan until just cooked, then drain and flake the flesh. Mix the breadcrumbs into the Marvel with seasoning, half the cheese and the mustard. Cook the mixture over a low heat for a few minutes. Arrange the fish in a flameproof dish and pour over the hot Marvel mixture. Scatter the remaining cheese on top and grill until golden. Serve with a crisp green salad.

Fish Florentine

Serves 4

Metric		Imperial
920 (230)	CALORIES	**920 (230)**
450 g	**white fish fillet**	1 lb
25 g	**Outline**	1 oz
	grated rind and juice of $\frac{1}{2}$ lemon	
	salt and pepper	
1 tablespoon	**flour**	1 tablespoon
300 ml	**made-up Marvel**	$\frac{1}{2}$ pint
2 (227-g) packets	**frozen chopped spinach, thawed, or**	2 (8-oz) packets
450 g	**fresh leaf spinach**	1 lb
2	**large tomatoes**	2
25 g	**Edam cheese, grated**	1 oz
1 dessertspoon	**fresh Slimcea breadcrumbs**	1 dessertspoon

Skin the fish and cut into bite-sized pieces. Melt the Outline in a frying pan and sauté the fish until the flesh is firm. Add the lemon rind and juice and seasoning to taste and continue cooking for a further 5 minutes. Transfer the fish to a plate. Add the flour to the Outline left in the pan and cook, stirring, for 1 minute. Gradually stir in the Marvel and bring to the boil, stirring continuously. Return the fish to the sauce. Taste and adjust the seasoning if necessary.

Drain the frozen spinach thoroughly. If using fresh spinach cook in very little salted water until tender. Drain well and chop. Season with pepper and arrange in an ovenproof dish. Peel and thinly slice the tomatoes and arrange over the spinach. Spoon the fish mixture over the top. Mix the cheese and breadcrumbs together and sprinkle over the top. Bake in a moderately hot oven (200°C, 400°F, Gas Mark 6) for 15-20 minutes until golden brown.

Seafood Special

See photograph on page 2
Serves 4

Metric		Imperial
900 (225)	CALORIES	**900 (225)**
4	**fillets of plaice**	4
	salt and pepper	
1 (340-g) can	**asparagus spears**	1 (12-oz) can
15 g	**Outline**	$\frac{1}{2}$ oz
100 g	**peeled prawns**	4 oz
	few drops lemon juice	
150 ml	**mixed half dry white wine and half water**	$\frac{1}{4}$ pint
4	**white peppercorns**	4
2	**bay leaves**	2
25 g	**dry Marvel**	1 oz
1 tablespoon	**cornflour**	1 tablespoon
	Garnish	
1 tablespoon	**chopped parsley**	1 tablespoon
	twists of lemon	

Skin the fish and season well. Divide the asparagus into four portions and roll a portion in each fish fillet. Secure each roll with a wooden cocktail stick. Lightly grease an ovenproof dish with the Outline and arrange the rolls in it. Scatter the prawns over the top. Sprinkle with lemon juice, wine mixture, peppercorns and bay leaves, cover and cook in a moderate oven (180°C, 350°F, Gas Mark 4) for 30-40 minutes. Lift out the fish rolls and prawns, remove the cocktail sticks and set aside on a serving dish. Keep warm.

Strain the fish liquid and stir in the Marvel. Mix the cornflour with a little of the liquid then stir in the rest. Bring to the boil, stirring continuously until thickened. Taste and adjust the seasoning if necessary. Pour the sauce over the fish rolls, sprinkle with parsley and garnish with twists of lemon.

Serve with a crisp green salad and, if the daily calorie allowance permits, a few new potatoes for a special occasion meal.

Swiss Herrings

See photograph on page 49
Serves 4

Metric		Imperial
1320 (330)	CALORIES	**1320 (330)**
4	**herrings**	4
1 tablespoon	**French mustard**	1 tablespoon
	salt and pepper	
25 g	**Outline, melted**	1 oz
4	**slices processed Gruyère cheese**	4
	Garnish	
	few sprigs parsley	
	lemon wedges	

Wash and gut the herrings, clean and remove the heads. Split the fish and place flat with skin uppermost on a clean surface and press out the backbone. Spread a little mustard over the flesh and season well.

Fold the fish to enclose the mustard and make three slits in the skin on both sides of each fish. Brush with the Outline. Grill the fish for 5 minutes then turn it over and grill for 5 minutes more. Put a slice of Gruyère on each fish and continue to grill gently until the cheese has melted and the fish is completely cooked. Serve garnished with a few sprigs of parsley and lemon wedges.

Stuffed Peppers

See photograph on page 1
Serves 4

Metric		Imperial
400 (100)	CALORIES	**400 (100)**
25 g	**Outline**	1 oz
1	**onion, finely chopped**	1
350 g	**raw chicken meat, cut into bite–sized pieces**	12 oz
225 g	**button mushrooms, sliced**	8 oz
1 (283-g) can	**beansprouts**	1 (10-oz) can
4	**tomatoes, peeled**	4
	salt and pepper	
2 tablespoons	**chopped parsley**	2 tablespoons
1 tablespoon	**soy sauce**	1 tablespoon
4	**red or green peppers**	4
4 teaspoons	**Marvel Yogurt (see page 98)**	4 teaspoons

Melt the Outline in a pan, add the onion and chicken. Cook, stirring, until the onion is soft and the chicken firm. Remove from the heat and stir in the mushrooms and beansprouts. Roughly chop the tomatoes and add to the mixture together with a little seasoning, the parsley and soy sauce.

Cut the tops off the peppers and remove the seeds and any pith from inside. Cut a very little off the base of the peppers in order to stand them up. Blanch the peppers and their tops in boiling water for a few minutes. Drain well on absorbent kitchen paper. Carefully stuff the peppers with the chicken mixture. Place in a greased ovenproof dish and replace their tops. Alternatively, the tops may be chopped and incorporated in the filling. Cover with foil and cook in a moderate oven (180°C, 350°F, Gas Mark 4) for 30-40 minutes or until the peppers and their filling are cooked. Serve topped with a little yogurt.

Orange Parsley Chicken

See photograph on page 52
Serves 4

Metric		Imperial
1720 (430)	CALORIES	**1720 (430)**
50 g	**Outline**	2 oz
2 tablespoons	**chopped parsley**	2 tablespoons
	juice of 2 oranges	
	salt and pepper	
1 (326-g) can	**sweetcorn kernels**	1 (11½-oz) can
5 tablespoons	**Slimcea breadcrumbs**	5 tablespoons
1	**onion, finely chopped**	1
1 tablespoon	**dried parsley**	1 tablespoon
1 teaspoon	**dried thyme, or**	1 teaspoon
2 tablespoons	**chopped fresh parsley and thyme mixed**	2 tablespoons
1	**egg yolk**	1
1 (weighing about 1 kg)	**small roasting chicken**	1 (weighing about 2 lb)
	Garnish	
	sprigs of watercress	

Melt the Outline in a small saucepan and mix in the parsley and the orange juice. Season to taste. Drain the sweetcorn and mix 2 tablespoons with the Slimcea breadcrumbs, herbs and egg yolk. Use this mixture to stuff the chicken. Put the chicken in a roasting tin and pour over the orange mixture. Cook in a moderately hot oven (190°C, 375°F, Gas Mark 5) for about 1-1¼ hours, basting frequently. Heat the remaining sweetcorn and serve around the chicken. Garnish with a small bunch of watercress.

Turkey in Mushroom Sauce

Serves 4

Metric		Imperial
1160 (290)	CALORIES	**1160 (290)**
1	**large onion, chopped**	1
450 ml	**dry cider**	$\frac{3}{4}$ pint
25 g	**Outline**	1 oz
175 g	**mushrooms, sliced**	6 oz
15 g	**flour**	$\frac{1}{2}$ oz
$\frac{1}{2}$ teaspoon	**prepared mustard**	$\frac{1}{2}$ teaspoon
	salt and pepper	
450 g	**cooked turkey or chicken meat, diced**	1 lb
2 tablespoons	**soured cream**	2 tablespoons
	Garnish	
	chopped parsley	

Place the onion in a saucepan with the cider and simmer for 10 minutes.

Melt the Outline in another saucepan and sauté the mushrooms for 3 minutes. Stir in the flour and cook for 1 minute. Gradually stir in the cider and onion, stirring continuously until the sauce is smooth and thickened. Stir in the mustard and season to taste. Add the turkey and reheat to boiling point. Simmer for 2 minutes then stir in the soured cream. Serve sprinkled with chopped parsley and accompanied by a green vegetable or salad.

Turkey Escalopes with Mint

See photograph on page 50
Serves 4

Metric		Imperial
1160 (290)	CALORIES	**1320 (330)**
4 (100-g)	**slices uncooked turkey breast**	4 (4-oz)
1 tablespoon	**seasoned flour**	1 tablespoon
50 g	**Outline**	2 oz
150 ml	**chicken stock (made with a stock cube)**	$\frac{1}{4}$ pint
1 teaspoon	**vinegar**	1 teaspoon
1 tablespoon	**mint jelly**	1 tablespoon
	salt and pepper	
100 g	**green ribbon noodles**	4 oz
	Garnish	
	few sprigs mint	

Place the turkey breast between two pieces of damp greaseproof paper and beat out as thinly as possible. Dust with the flour. Melt half the Outline in a frying pan and fry the escalopes, two at a time, until golden on both sides. Add a little more of the Outline if needed, but reserve 15 g/½ oz for the noodles. Keep the cooked turkey slices hot.

Add the stock, vinegar and mint jelly to the juices left in the pan and stir over a low heat until the jelly has melted. Adjust the seasoning to taste then bring to the boil and simmer for 1 minute. Meanwhile cook the noodles in boiling salted water until tender, about 12 minutes. Drain and toss in the remaining Outline. Arrange the noodles around the edge of a heated serving dish, place the turkey slices in the middle and pour over the sauce. Garnish with the mint. This dish may be accompanied by a side dish of sliced oranges and tomatoes.

Spring Chicken

Serves 4

Metric		Imperial
920 (230)	CALORIES	**920 (230)**
4 (weighing about 250 g each)	**chicken joints, skinned**	4 (weighing about 9 oz each)
	salt and pepper	
1	**bay leaf**	1
	pinch of dried mixed herbs	
1	**onion, halved**	1
600 ml	**chicken stock (made with a stock cube)**	1 pint
15 g	**Outline**	½ oz
15 g	**flour**	½ oz
1 teaspoon	**curry powder**	1 teaspoon
3 heaped tablespoons	**dry Marvel**	3 heaped tablespoons
50 g	**frozen peas**	2 oz
2	**spring onions, chopped**	2
150 ml	**Marvel Yogurt (see page 98)**	¼ pint

Season the chicken joints with salt and pepper and grill for 5 minutes on each side. Place in a heavy saucepan or flameproof casserole with the bay leaf, herbs, onion and stock. Bring to the boil, cover and simmer for about 45 minutes or until the chicken is cooked.

Melt the Outline in a saucepan and stir in the flour and curry powder. Cook, stirring, for a few minutes. Drain the stock from the chicken and keep the chicken hot. Stir the Marvel into the stock and gradually stir into the curry-flavoured roux. Bring to the boil, stirring continuously. Add the peas and cook gently until tender, about 4 minutes. Add the spring onions to the sauce and allow to cool a little. Stir in the yogurt and pour over the chicken. Serve with a green salad or vegetable.

Easy Paella

Serves 4

Metric		Imperial
1560 (390)	CALORIES	**1560 (390)**
25 g	**Outline**	1 oz
1	**small onion, chopped**	1
1 clove	**garlic, crushed**	1 clove
350 g	**cooked chicken meat, diced**	12 oz
600 ml	**chicken stock (made with a stock cube)**	1 pint
175 g	**long-grain rice**	6 oz
100 g	**pimiento, chopped**	4 oz
3	**tomatoes, peeled and quartered**	3
½ teaspoon	**ground turmeric**	½ teaspoon
	salt and pepper	
100 g	**peeled prawns**	4 oz
100 g	**shelled mussels**	4 oz
50 g	**frozen peas**	2 oz

Melt the Outline in a large frying pan and gently fry the onion and garlic until soft but not browned. Stir in the chicken and cook for a few minutes. Stir in the stock, rice, pimiento and tomatoes. Add the turmeric and season generously. Bring to the boil, cover and simmer for 25 minutes or until most of the stock is abosrbed and the rice tender. Taste and adjust the seasoning if necessary then stir in the remaining ingredients and cook gently for a further 5 minutes. Serve with a salad or green beans.

Mushroom and Tomato Stuffing

Makes sufficient to stuff 1 large chicken

Metric		Imperial
470	CALORIES	**470**
175 g	**mushrooms, chopped**	6 oz
175 g	**tomatoes, peeled and chopped**	6 oz
½ teaspoon	**dried mixed herbs**	½ teaspoon
	salt and pepper	
	pinch of grated nutmeg	
5 tablespoons	**Slimcea breadcrumbs**	5 tablespoons

Mix all the ingredients together and use to stuff a large chicken or small turkey.

Crunchy Haddock Casserole (see page 40); Fish Knots (see page 41); Swiss Herrings (see page 44)

Curried Chicken with Fruit

Serves 6

Metric		Imperial
1860 (310)	CALORIES	**1860 (310)**
50 g	**Outline**	2 oz
1	**onion, chopped**	1
1–2 tablespoons	**curry powder**	1–2 tablespoons
1 tablespoon	**plain flour**	1 tablespoon
600 ml	**chicken stock (made with a stock cube)**	1 pint
575 g	**cooked chicken meat**	1¼ lb
2 tablespoons	**mango chutney**	2 tablespoons
1	**apple, peeled, cored and chopped**	1
	salt and pepper	
50 g	**dry Marvel**	2 oz
1 (227-g) can	**pineapple in natural juice, drained**	1 (8-oz) can
100 g	**courgettes, sliced**	4 oz
1	**banana, sliced**	1

Melt the Outline in a large saucepan and sauté the onion until soft but not browned. Stir in the curry powder to taste and flour, cook for a few minutes then gradually stir in half the stock. Bring to the boil, stirring continuously. Cut the chicken into bite-sized pieces and add to the curry mixture. Stir in the chutney and apple, season to taste, cover and simmer for 15 minutes. Dissolve the Marvel in the remaining warm stock, and add to the curry with the pineapple, courgettes and banana. Cover and simmer for a further 5 minutes. Adjust the seasoning and serve with a salad or green beans, or if the diet allows, a little plain boiled rice.

Previous pages *Noisettes of Lamb with Pineapple (see page 59); Turkey Escalopes with Mint (see page 46)*
Carrot and Cucumber Vichy (see page 66); Orange Parsley Chicken (see page 45)

Chicken with Watercress Stuffing

Serves 4

Metric		Imperial
1520 (380)	CALORIES	**1520 (380)**
1 (1.5-kg)	**roasting chicken**	1 (3-lb)
	Stuffing	
1	**small onion, chopped**	1
2	**sticks celery, chopped**	2
50 g	**Outline, melted**	2 oz
	salt and pepper	
2	**bunches watercress, stalks removed and chopped**	2
5 tablespoons	**Slimcea breadcrumbs**	5 tablespoons
1	**egg**	1

First prepare the stuffing. Mix all the ingredients together, binding them with the beaten egg. Use the mixture to stuff the chicken. Place the chicken in a roasting tin, cover with foil and roast in a moderately hot oven (190°C, 375°F, Gas Mark 5) for approximately $1\frac{1}{4}$ hours. Remove the foil for the last 15 minutes of cooking time for the skin to brown.

Savoy Special

Serves 4

Metric		Imperial
1160 (290)	CALORIES	**1160 (290)**
6	**large outer leaves from a Savoy cabbage**	6
225 g	**lean minced beef**	8 oz
1	**onion, sliced**	1
1 clove	**garlic, crushed**	1 clove
1 (425-g) can	**tomatoes**	1 (15-oz) can
	salt and pepper	
	Sauce	
25 g	**Outline**	1 oz
25 g	**flour**	1 oz
300 ml	**made-up Marvel**	$\frac{1}{2}$ pint
75 g	**Edam cheese, grated**	3 oz

Blanch the cabbage leaves in boiling salted water for about 5 minutes or until just tender. Drain well and cut out any pieces of thick stalk. Brown the mince over gentle heat without any extra fat, stirring continuously, in a non-stick or heavy-based saucepan. Add the onion and garlic and stir in the tomatoes. Season to taste, bring to the boil and simmer for 10 minutes.

Prepare an all-in-one sauce using the Outline, flour and Marvel (see page 111). Season well. Add most of the cheese. Layer the meat sauce, cabbage and cheese sauce in an ovenproof dish, finishing with a layer of cheese sauce. Sprinkle over the remaining cheese and cook in a moderately hot oven (190°C, 375°F, Gas Mark 5) for 25-30 minutes or until golden brown and bubbling hot.

Sicilian Veal Roast

Serves 8

Metric		Imperial
2400 (300)	CALORIES (see note)	2640 (330)
25 g	**Outline**	1 oz
	grated rind and juice of 1 large lemon	
	salt and pepper	
3 tablespoons	**Slimcea breadcrumbs**	3 tablespoons
1	**small onion, finely chopped**	1
1 tablespoon	**dried parsley**	1 tablespoon
½ teaspoon	**dried thyme or**	½ teaspoon
2 tablespoons	**chopped fresh parsley and thyme mixed**	2 tablespoons
1	**egg yolk**	1
1 teaspoon	**dried fennel seeds**	1 teaspoon
1 (weighing about 1 kg)	**small shoulder of veal, boned**	1 (weighing about 2¼ lb)
1 tablespoon	**flour**	1 tablespoon
300 ml	**chicken stock (made with a stock cube)**	½ pint
	Garnish	
	wedges of lemon	
	sprigs of watercress	

Melt the Outline in a small saucepan and stir in the lemon rind, juice and seasoning to taste. Mix half with the Slimcea breadcrumbs, onion, herbs, egg yolk and fennel seeds.

Place the veal, skin side down, on a board and spread with the stuffing. Roll up tightly and tie in three places with strong thread. Place in a roasting tin and brush with the reserved lemon mixture. Cook in a moderate oven (180°C, 350°F, Gas Mark 4) for 2 hours. Transfer to a heated serving dish and remove the thread. Garnish with lemon wedges and sprigs of watercress.

Mix the flour into the juices left in the roasting tin, stir well and cook for 1 minute. Gradually stir in the stock. Continue stirring over a moderate heat until the mixture boils and becomes thick and smooth. Serve this sauce separately with the veal roast.

Serve 100 g/4 oz of sliced veal to each person and accompany it with green salad and 75 g/3 oz each tiny boiled potatoes.

Note: *Allowing 100 g/4 oz meat and one eighth stuffing per portion.*

Worcestershire Beef

Serves 4

Metric		Imperial
1200 (300)	CALORIES	**1200 (300)**
450 g	**quick-fry steak**	1 lb
15 g	**Outline**	$\frac{1}{2}$ oz
2	**small onions, sliced**	2
1 clove	**garlic, crushed**	1 clove
1	**beef stock cube, crumbled**	1
150 ml	**boiling water**	$\frac{1}{4}$ pint
225 g	**button mushrooms, sliced**	8 oz
2 teaspoons	**Worcestershire sauce**	2 teaspoons
	salt and pepper	
50 g	**dry Marvel**	2 oz
1 tablespoon	**lemon juice**	1 tablespoon
	Garnish	
	chopped parsley	

Trim any fat from the meat and cut into thin strips. Melt the Outline in a frying pan, add the onion, garlic and meat and cook until the meat is browned and the onion soft. Dissolve the stock cube in the boiling water and stir into the meat together with the mushrooms, Worcestershire sauce and seasoning if necessary. Cover and simmer for 10 minutes. Mix the Marvel with just enough water to make a smooth mixture, add the lemon juice and stir into the meat away from the heat. Heat again without boiling. Garnish with the parsley. This dish would look attractive served surrounded by cut French beans.

Kebabs

See photograph on page 61
Serves 4-6

Metric		Imperial
1620 (405-270)	CALORIES	**1620 (405-270)**
900 g	**lean lamb**	2 lb
150 ml	**Marvel Yogurt (see page 98)**	$\frac{1}{4}$ pint
1 tablespoon	**oil**	1 tablespoon
1 tablespoon	**lemon juice**	1 tablespoon
	salt and pepper	
	few sprigs fresh rosemary or marjoram	

Cut the meat into even-sized cubes, trimming off any fat. Whisk the yogurt with the oil, lemon juice and seasoning to taste. Place the meat in a shallow dish, sprinkle over the herbs and pour on the yogurt mixture. Cover and leave to marinate for several hours or overnight in the refrigerator.

Remove the meat from the marinade and thread it on to skewers. Grill for at least 10 minutes on each side or until cooked to taste. Use the marinade to baste the meat frequently during cooking.

Serve with a crisp mixed green salad. Halved small tomatoes, whole small onions and mushrooms may be threaded on the skewers with the meat.

Saffron Lamb

Serves 4

Metric		Imperial
1180 (295)	CALORIES	**1180 (295)**
4	**lean lamb chops**	4
50 g	**mushrooms, chopped**	2 oz
1 clove	**garlic, crushed**	1 clove
	a few strands of saffron	
50 g	**dry Marvel**	2 oz
3 tablespoons	**water**	3 tablespoons
1 teaspoon	**lemon juice**	1 teaspoon
	salt and pepper	
4	**tomatoes**	4

Trim any excess fat from the chops and grill for 8-10 minutes on each side.

Mix the mushrooms, garlic, saffron and Marvel with the water and lemon juice. Season generously. Spread the mushroom mixture on top of the hot chops. Halve the tomatoes, season well and arrange in the grill pan. Grill for about 5 minutes or until the mushroom mixture is hot and bubbling. Garnish each chop with the grilled tomatoes before serving.

57

Layered Lamb Bake

See photograph on page 62
Serves 4-5

Metric		Imperial
1180 (280–235)	CALORIES	**1180 (280–235)**
225 g	cooked lean lamb	8 oz
1	onion, grated	1
150 ml	beef stock (made with a stock cube)	$\frac{1}{4}$ pint
1 tablespoon	tomato purée	1 tablespoon
1 teaspoon	dried oregano	1 teaspoon
1 teaspoon	Worcestershire sauce	1 teaspoon
	salt and pepper	
225 g	par-boiled carrots	8 oz
225 g	par-boiled potatoes	8 oz
50 g	dry Marvel	2 oz
1	egg	1
75 g	Edam cheese, grated	3 oz
	grated nutmeg	

Mince the lamb and mix well with the onion, stock, tomato purée, oregano, Worcestershire sauce and seasoning to taste. Slice the vegetables thinly and layer them in the dish with the meat mixture. Beat the Marvel with the egg and 300 ml/$\frac{1}{2}$ pint water (if possible use that from the vegetables). Reserve a little of the cheese and add the remainder to the egg. Season to taste and pour the mixture over the dish. Sprinkle with nutmeg and the reserved cheese. Cook in a moderate oven (180°C, 350°F, Gas Mark 4) for 45 minutes, until cooked and browned. Serve with a green vegetable.

Oven Chops Italienne

Serves 4

Metric		Imperial
880 (220)	CALORIES	**880 (220)**
25 g	Outline	1 oz
1	large onion, thinly sliced into rings	1
4	lean lamb chops	4
225 g	mushrooms, chopped	8 oz
1 (227-g) can	tomatoes	1 (8-oz) can
	salt and pepper	
	generous pinch of dried oregano	
15 g	grated Parmesan cheese	$\frac{1}{2}$ oz

Melt the Outline in a frying pan and sauté the onion until softened. Remove the onion from the pan and cook the chops rapidly on both sides to seal.

Arrange the chops in an ovenproof dish with the onion and mushrooms. Pour over the tomatoes and season well with salt, pepper and oregano. Cover the dish and cook in a moderately hot oven (190°C, 375°F, Gas Mark 5) for approximately 45 minutes. Remove the lid, sprinkle the top with the cheese and cook for a further 15 minutes. Serve with small jacket potatoes and braised celery.

Noisettes of Lamb with Pineapple

Serves 4

Metric		Imperial
2400 (600) if lean and fat eaten	CALORIES	if lean and fat eaten **2400 (600)**
1400 (350) if lean only eaten		if lean only eaten **1400 (350)**
25 g	**Outline**	1 oz
1 teaspoon	**runny honey**	1 teaspoon
1 teaspoon	**dry mustard**	1 teaspoon
1 clove	**garlic, crushed**	1 clove
2 tablespoons	**chopped parsley**	2 tablespoons
1 (227-g) can	**pineapple rings in natural juice**	1 (8-oz) can
	salt and pepper	
8	**noisettes of lamb, tied with strong thread**	8
	Garnish	
	few sprigs of watercress	

Melt the Outline in a small pan and stir in the honey, mustard, garlic and parsley. Add the juice from the can of pineapple and seasoning to taste.

Arrange the noisettes in the grill pan and brush them with some of the Outline mixture. Grill for 5-6 minutes on each side, basting frequently with the mixture until golden brown and cooked through.

Cut the pineapple rings in half and heat gently in the remaining Outline mixture. Arrange the noisettes on a heated serving dish with the pineapple and sprigs of watercress. The remaining sauce may be spooned over the top or served separately.

Serve two noisettes to each person with 100 g/4 oz broccoli. Cut the fat away from the noisettes of lamb if your calorie allowance does not allow for this.

Pizza Deliziosa

See photograph opposite
Serves 4

Metric		Imperial
1160 (290)	CALORIES	**1160 (290)**
15 g	**Outline**	$\frac{1}{2}$ oz
1	**onion, chopped**	1
100 g	**mushrooms, chopped**	4 oz
2 tablespoons	**tomato purée**	2 tablespoons
1 teaspoon	**dried oregano**	1 teaspoon
	salt and pepper	
25 g	**black olives, stoned**	1 oz
100 g	**self-raising flour**	4 oz
	pinch of salt	
$\frac{1}{2}$ teaspoon	**baking powder**	$\frac{1}{2}$ teaspoon
$\frac{1}{2}$ teaspoon	**dried mixed herbs**	$\frac{1}{2}$ teaspoon
25 g	**Outline**	1 oz
4 tablespoons	**made-up Marvel**	4 tablespoons
75 g	**Edam cheese, grated**	3 oz
50 g	**garlic sausage, thinly sliced**	2 oz
2	**tomatoes, sliced**	2

First prepare the topping. Melt the 15 g/$\frac{1}{2}$ oz Outline in a small saucepan. Add the onion and cook, stirring occasionally, until soft but not browned. Add the mushrooms, tomato purée and oregano and season to taste. Reserve one olive and chop the remainder. Add to the onion mixture. Leave to cool.

Prepare the base by sifting the flour, salt and baking powder into a bowl. Add the herbs and rub in the Outline until the mixture resembles fine breadcrumbs. Stir in the Marvel to form a soft dough. Knead lightly on a floured surface and roll out to form a round of approximately 25 cm/10 inches in diameter. Place on a greased baking tray or pizza plate and pinch up the edges of the dough to form a slight rim.

Spread the onion mixture over the dough and sprinkle most of the cheese on top. Arrange the garlic sausage and tomato on top and sprinkle over the remaining grated cheese.

Top with the remaining olive and bake in a moderately hot oven (200°C, 400°F, Gas Mark 6) for 25 minutes or until cooked.

Kebabs (see page 56); Pizza Deliziosa (see above)

Gingered Kidney Casserole

See photograph opposite
Serves 4

Metric		Imperial
720 (180)	CALORIES	**720 (180)**
450 g	**ox kidney**	1 lb
50 g	**Outline**	2 oz
300 ml	**low-calorie dry ginger ale**	$\frac{1}{2}$ pint
1 tablespoon	**grated root ginger**	1 tablespoon
$\frac{1}{2}$ teaspoon	**ground ginger**	$\frac{1}{2}$ teaspoon
	salt and pepper	
1 tablespoon	**vinegar**	1 tablespoon
1	**beef stock cube, crumbled**	1
1 tablespoon	**low-calorie blackcurrant jam**	1 tablespoon
1 tablespoon	**cornflour**	1 tablespoon
2 tablespoons	**water**	2 tablespoons
	Garnish	
1 tablespoon	**chopped parsley**	1 tablespoon

Trim the kidneys, remove the hard cores and cut into pieces. Melt the Outline in a large saucepan. Sauté the kidney gently until sealed and golden on all sides. Add the ginger ale, root ginger, ground ginger, seasoning, vinegar and crumbled stock cube and bring to the boil, stirring continuously.

Cover and simmer for 30–40 minutes or until the kidney is tender. Stir in the jam and stir until melted. Mix the cornflour with the water, mix in a little of the cooking liquid and return to the pan. Bring to the boil, stirring continuously. Adjust the seasoning and serve garnished with chopped parsley and 100 g/4 oz steamed cauliflower per person.

Layered Lamb Bake (see page 58); Gingered Kidney Casserole (see above)

Barbecued Spareribs

Serves 4

Metric		Imperial
1200 (300)	CALORIES	**1200 (300)**
675 g	**pork spareribs**	1½ lb
25 g	**Outline**	1 oz
	Sauce	
2 tablespoons	**tomato purée**	2 tablespoons
¼ teaspoon	**Hermesetas Liquid Sweetener**	¼ teaspoon
1 clove	**garlic, crushed**	1 clove
½ teaspoon	**ground ginger**	½ teaspoon
½ teaspoon	**prepared mustard**	½ teaspoon
½ teaspoon	**Worcestershire sauce**	½ teaspoon
	salt and pepper	

Trim any excess fat from the spareribs and cut between the bones to separate them. Melt the Outline in a deep frying pan, add the spareribs and cook, turning frequently until well browned all over.

Mix together all the ingredients for the sauce and make up to 300 ml/½ pint with water. Remove the spareribs from the heat and very carefully add the sauce. Bring to the boil, cover and simmer gently for 50-60 minutes. Turn the spareribs frequently during cooking. The sauce should be greatly reduced and thickened by the end of the cooking time.

Hawaiian Gammon Rashers

Serves 4

Metric		Imperial
960 (240)	CALORIES	**960 (240)**
4 (100-g)	**lean gammon rashers**	4 (4-oz)
15 g	**Outline**	½ oz
1 teaspoon	**French mustard**	1 teaspoon
	salt and pepper	
1 (227-g) can	**pineapple rings in natural juice, drained**	1 (8-oz) can
½	**bunch watercress**	½
150 ml	**Marvel Yogurt (see page 98)**	¼ pint

Trim the gammon rashers, removing any fat. Mix together the Outline, mustard and seasoning and spread this mixture over the gammon.

Grill the gammon for about 7-10 minutes on each side, top each rasher with a pineapple ring and reheat for 2-3 minutes. Finely chop all but a few sprigs of the watercress and mix with the yogurt. Season generously and spoon a little over each piece of pineapple on the gammon. Serve the remainder in a small side dish. Garnish the dish with the reserved watercress.

Baked Liver Loaf

Serves 6

Metric		Imperial
1080 (180)	CALORIES	**1080 (180)**
25 g	**Outline**	1 oz
1 clove	**garlic, crushed**	1 clove
1	**onion, roughly chopped**	1
450 g	**ox liver, roughly chopped**	1 lb
	salt and pepper	
3	**slices Slimcea**	3
1	**egg**	1
150 ml	**made-up Marvel**	$\frac{1}{4}$ pint
2 teaspoons	**prepared mustard**	2 teaspoons

Melt the Outline in a frying pan, add the garlic, onion and liver. Season well and cook, stirring until the liver changes colour and the onion is soft. Allow to cool slightly then mince finely or liquidise with the Slimcea and mix in the beaten egg, Marvel, seasoning and mustard. Place the mixture in a non-stick 0.5-kg/1-lb loaf tin. Stand the tin in a pan of hot water and bake in a moderate oven (180°C, 350°F, Gas Mark 4) for 1 hour or until firm to the touch and lightly browned on top.

Vegetables and salads

Vegetables and salads are the great stand-by of all slimmers. They are filling and extremely low in calories. The only exceptions are avocado pears and potatoes. The former contain a great deal of fat and the latter are almost always eaten in large portion sizes or mixed with fat during preparation. But do remember that potatoes are very nutritious, and if you want to make a meal of them occasionally then do so. A large jacket potato baked with prawns or other fish, or 25 g/1 oz grated cheese or some chopped lean meat will provide about 250 Calories. As a vegetable accompaniment to a meal that would be rather high, but as a meal in its own right it is very modest.

Remember too that onions and mushrooms absorb huge amounts of fat if they're fried, so eat them raw, cooked in stock or sautéed in a little Outline. The trouble with the low-calorie vegetables is that they become very boring if they're just plain boiled. And the moment you try to cheer up lettuce leaves with dressing, the calorie content shoots through the roof. But the recipes for Yogurt Dressing and Slimmers' Mayonnaise should help.

Try mixing vegetables to make them more interesting – mushrooms and onions with all the green vegetables, peppers with corn and peas, celery with cabbage. And use vegetables you don't normally eat bean sprouts, chicory, aubergines and fennel.

If you're cutting down on fatty gravy try adding lemon yogurt to vegetables to make the meal moist. The recipe for Baked Vegetables with Spiced Yogurt will start you off in the right direction. Add different flavours to salads – mint, rosemary, chives, and use salads as a second vegetable – they take a long time to eat!

Carrot and Cucumber Vichy

Serves 4

Metric		Imperial
180 (45)	CALORIES	**180 (45)**
1	large cucumber	1
225 g	carrots	8 oz
15 g	Outline	$\frac{1}{2}$ oz
	salt and pepper	
1 drop	Hermesetas Liquid Sweetener	1 drop
2 teaspoons	chopped parsley or chives	2 teaspoons

Peel the cucumber, halve lengthways and cut across in 1-cm/$\frac{1}{2}$-inch slices. Blanch in boiling salted water for 1 minute, drain, rinse and set aside. Quarter the carrots lengthways and place in a saucepan with the Outline, salt and enough water to just cover. Bring to the boil, cover and cook until tender, about 10 minutes. Remove the lid and cook fairly rapidly until most of the water has evaporated. Add the cucumber, carrots and Hermesetas and season to taste. Toss the vegetables until well coated in the glaze left in the pan. Serve sprinkled with the chives or parsley.

Baked Vegetables with Spiced Yogurt

See photograph on page 71
Serves 6

Metric		Imperial
420 (70)	CALORIES	**420 (70)**
25 g	**Outline**	1 oz
1	**small onion, chopped**	1
1	**head celery, sliced**	1
1	**green pepper, seeds removed and chopped**	1
4	**cloves garlic, crushed**	4
1 teaspoon	**dill seeds**	1 teaspoon
1 teaspoon	**turmeric**	1 teaspoon
1 teaspoon	**curry powder**	1 teaspoon
1 teaspoon	**chilli powder**	1 teaspoon
2 teaspoons	**ground coriander**	2 teaspoons
	few drops Hermesetas Liquid Sweetener	
	salt and pepper	
300 ml	**Marvel Yogurt (see page 98)**	$\frac{1}{2}$ pint
2 tablespoons	**tomato purée**	2 tablespoons
1	**medium marrow**	1
	Garnish	
1	**green pepper**	1
1	**lemon**	1

Melt the Outline in a saucepan, add the onion, celery, green pepper and garlic. Cook, stirring, for about 5 minutes or until the vegetables are softened. Add the dill seeds, spices and Hermesetas. Season generously and cook, stirring continuously over a low heat, for a further 5 minutes. Remove from the heat and stir in the yogurt and tomato purée.

Halve the marrow and scoop out the seeds. Place the marrow in an ovenproof dish and divide the curry mixture between the two halves. Cover loosely with foil and bake in a moderate oven (180°C, 350°F, Gas Mark 4) for about 1 hour or until the marrow is tender. Garnish with halved slices of green pepper and lemon wedges.

Leeks Provençale

Serves 4

Metric		Imperial
280 (70)	CALORIES	**280 (70)**
4	**medium leeks**	4
25 g	**Outline**	1 oz
1	**clove garlic, crushed**	1
1 (227-g) can	**tomatoes**	1 (8-oz) can
	salt and pepper	
3 drops	**Hermesetas Liquid Sweetener**	3 drops
1 tablespoon	**lemon juice**	1 tablespoon
2 tablespoons	**chopped parsley**	2 tablespoons

Wash and trim the leeks. Melt the Outline in a deep frying pan. Add the leeks and garlic and cook, turning frequently until the leeks are soft on the outside. Stir in the tomatoes and season to taste. Add the Hermesetas and lemon juice, cover and cook gently for 15 minutes or until the leeks are tender. Stir in the parsley just before serving. Serve hot or allow to cool and chill before serving.

American Salad

Serves 4

Metric		Imperial
960 (240)	CALORIES	**960 (240)**
3	**rashers lean bacon**	3
50 g	**Cheddar cheese, diced**	2 oz
1	**small onion, chopped**	1
225 g	**fresh leaf spinach, finely shredded**	8 oz
4 tablespoons	**Slimcea Croûtons (see page 38)**	4 tablespoons
	Dressing	
150 ml	**Marvel Yogurt (see page 98)**	$\frac{1}{4}$ pint
1 clove	**garlic, crushed**	1 clove
1 tablespoon	**lemon juice**	1 tablespoon
3 tablespoons	**tomato juice**	3 tablespoons
	salt and pepper	

Grill the bacon until crisp and chop roughly. Mix with the cheese, onion and spinach. Mix in half the croûtons.

Mix all the dressing ingredients together and pour over the salad. Toss lightly and sprinkle with the remaining croûtons.

Minted Courgette Salad

See photograph on page 72
Serves 4

Metric		Imperial
440 (110)	CALORIES	**440 (110)**
450 g	courgettes	1 lb
40 g	Outline	1½ oz
1 clove	garlic, crushed	1 clove
1	medium onion, thinly sliced	1
	salt and pepper	
2	large tomatoes	2
1 tablespoon	oil	1 tablespoon
1 tablespoon	vinegar	1 tablespoon
2 tablespoons	chopped mint	2 tablespoons

Trim the courgettes and thinly pare to remove about half the peel. Slice thinly.

Melt the Outline in a frying pan, add the garlic and onion and fry gently until the onion is transparent. Add the courgettes, season and cook for 2 minutes. Leave to cool.

Dip the tomatoes in boiling water for a few seconds. Remove and peel the tomatoes, remove the seeds and chop the flesh roughly.

Mix the oil and vinegar together and stir into the courgettes with the tomato. Serve in individual salad bowls, sprinkled with the chopped mint.

Cathcart Salad

Serves 4

Metric		Imperial
640 (160)	CALORIES	**640 (160)**
225 g	cottage cheese	8 oz
1 teaspoon	lemon juice	1 teaspoon
1 tablespoon	chopped fresh herbs (parsley, chives or thyme)	1 tablespoon
1	peach, peeled and chopped	1
1	small crisp lettuce	1
1	onion, chopped	1
4 tablespoons	Slimcea Croûtons (see page 38)	4 tablespoons
4	black olives, stoned and chopped	4

Mix the cottage cheese, lemon juice and herbs together. Add the peach. Shred the lettuce and place in a large bowl with the onion. Arrange the cottage cheese mixture on top. Mix the croûtons with the olives and sprinkle over the salad.

Patio Dip

See photograph on page 133
Serves 4

Metric		Imperial
440 (without vegetables or fruit)	CALORIES	(without vegetables or fruit) **440**
225 g	cottage cheese	8 oz
4 heaped tablespoons	dry Marvel	4 heaped tablespoons
1	small onion, quartered	1
½ teaspoon	curry paste	½ teaspoon
1 teaspoon	lemon juice	1 teaspoon
2 tablespoons	water	2 tablespoons
	salt and pepper	
	selection of prepared vegetables or fruit	
	Garnish	
	chopped parsley	

Place the cottage cheese, Marvel, onion, curry paste and lemon juice in a liquidiser and blend until smooth. Stir in the water and season to taste. Turn into a serving dish and chill. Serve surrounded by the vegetables or fruit which should be dipped into the mixture.

Kaleidoscope Salad

See photograph on page 74
Serves 4-6

Metric		Imperial
780 (195-130)	CALORIES	**780 (195-130)**
225 g	red cabbage	8 oz
½	green pepper	½
2	sharp dessert apples	2
225 g	cooked chicken meat	8 oz
25 g	walnut pieces	1 oz
150 ml	Piquant Dressing (see page 79)	¼ pint
	salt and pepper	
	Garnish	
	chopped parsley	

Shred the cabbage finely. Remove the seeds from the pepper, core the apples and roughly chop both ingredients. Cut the chicken into bite-sized pieces and toss in the dressing with the other ingredients. Adjust seasoning if necessary. Serve sprinkled with parsley.

Baked Vegetables with Spiced Yogurt (see page 67)

Pasta Salad with Fish

See photograph opposite
Serves 4

Metric		Imperial
1760 (440)	CALORIES	**1760 (440)**
225 g	**small pasta shapes**	8 oz
100 g	**button mushrooms**	4 oz
25 g	**Outline**	1 oz
1 (198-g) can	**tuna**	1 (7-oz) can
4 tablespoons	**Slimmers' Mayonnaise (see page 78)**	4 tablespoons
2	**spring onions, chopped**	2
2 tablespoons	**chopped parsley**	2 tablespoons
	salt and pepper	
4	**large lettuce leaves**	4
	Garnish	
1	**hard-boiled egg, chopped (optional)**	1

Cook the pasta in boiling salted water for about 12 minutes or until just tender. Drain and rinse in boiling water. Slice the mushrooms thinly. Melt the Outline in a small pan and toss the mushrooms in it. Mix the mushrooms with the hot pasta and leave to cool.

Drain the tuna and mix the liquid into the mayonnaise. Flake the tuna and mix with the pasta, mayonnaise, spring onions, parsley and seasoning to taste. Wash and drain the lettuce and use to line four individual bowls. Fill the lined bowls with the salad and garnish each with a little chopped egg if used.

Previous pages *Minted Courgette Salad (see page 69); Slimmers' Yogurt Dressing (see page 79); Fruit 'n' Vegetable Salad (see page 76); Greek Cheese Salad (see page 78); Slimmers' Mayonnaise (see page 78)*
Kaleidoscope Salad (see page 70); Piquant Dressing (see page 79); Pasta Salad with Fish (see above)

Sunny Rice Salad

Serves 6

Metric		Imperial
1240 (205)	CALORIES	**1240 (205)**
175 g	long-grain rice	6 oz
	generous pinch of powdered saffron or turmeric	
	salt	
275 g	cooked chicken meat	10 oz
100 g	cooked cod	4 oz
50 g	pimiento	2 oz
3	small gherkins	3
150 ml	Piquant Dressing (see page 79)	$\frac{1}{4}$ pint
	Garnish	
1 tablespoon	chopped parsley	1 tablespoon

Cook the rice with the saffron or turmeric in boiling salted water for about 15-20 minutes or until just tender. Drain and rinse with boiling water then leave to cool. Cut the chicken into bite-sized pieces and flake the cod. Chop the pimiento and gherkins and add to the rice together with the chicken and cod. Pour over the dressing and toss well. Sprinkle with chopped parsley before serving.

Fruit 'n' Vegetable Salad

See photograph on page 72
Serves 4

Metric		Imperial
320 (80)	CALORIES	**320 (80)**
2	oranges	2
2	large carrots, grated	2
2	dessert apples, cored and finely chopped	2
2 tablespoons	lemon juice	2 tablespoons
	Dressing	
50 g	cottage cheese	2 oz
	grated rind of 1 lemon	
	few drops Hermesetas Liquid Sweetener	
1 tablespoon	lemon juice	1 tablespoon
	salt and pepper	
	Garnish	
	chopped parsley or watercress	

Use a sharp knife to remove all the peel and pith from the oranges. Cut between each membrane and separate out the segments. Toss the carrots, apples and orange segments together in the lemon juice.

Liquidise the dressing ingredients together and spoon over the fruit and vegetable mixture. Garnish with the parsley or watercress.

Cheese and Tuna Salad

Serves 4

Metric		Imperial
1480 (370)	CALORIES	**1480 (370)**
1	**lettuce**	1
1	**small onion, thinly sliced**	1
$\frac{1}{2}$	**cucumber, diced**	$\frac{1}{2}$
3	**large tomatoes, chopped**	3
1	**bunch watercress, chopped**	1
1 (198-g) can	**tuna flaked**	1 (7-oz) can
100 g	**Gouda cheese, diced**	4 oz
4 tablespoons	**Slimcea Croûtons (see page 38)**	4 tablespoons
	Dressing	
2 tablespoons	**lemon juice**	2 tablespoons
4 tablespoons	**tomato juice**	4 tablespoons
1 teaspoon	**Worcestershire sauce**	1 teaspoon
	salt and pepper	
2 teaspoons	**chopped parsley or chives**	2 teaspoons

Tear the lettuce into pieces and place in a large salad bowl. Place all the remaining salad ingredients except the croûtons in a bowl and mix carefully.

Mix all the dressing ingredients together. Pour the dressing over the salad and toss well, then pile on the bed of lettuce. Sprinkle with the Slimcea Croûtons.

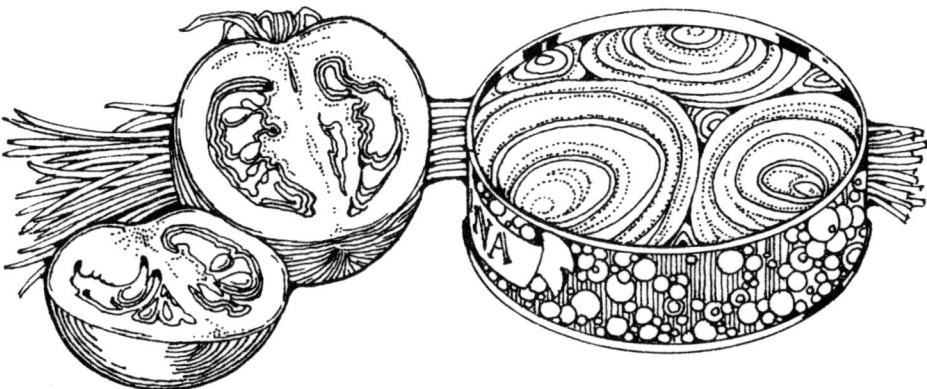

Greek Cheese Salad

See photograph on page 72
Serves 4

Metric		Imperial
520 (130)	CALORIES	**520 (130)**
1	lettuce	1
175 g	fetta cheese or	6 oz
225 g	cottage cheese	8 oz
2	medium tomatoes, peeled	2
2	slices Slimcea	2
25 g	Outline	1 oz
12	black olives, stoned	12
1 tablespoon	lemon juice	1 tablespoon
	salt and pepper	
	Garnish	
	grated rind of 2 lemons (optional)	

Trim the lettuce and use to line individual bowls. Crumble the fetta, if used, and chop the tomatoes, removing the seeds.

Cut the Slimcea into small croûtons. Melt the Outline in a small saucepan and fry the croûtons until golden.

Stir together the cheese, tomato, olives and lemon juice and season to taste. Divide between the bowls and top with the croûtons. Sprinkle with a little grated lemon rind.

Slimmers' Mayonnaise

See photograph on page 72
Serves 4

Metric		Imperial
160 (40)	CALORIES	**160 (40)**
2	hard-boiled egg yolks, sieved	2
1 tablespoon	vinegar	1 tablespoon
1 tablespoon	lemon juice	1 tablespoon
	salt and pepper	
	pinch of dry mustard	
$\frac{1}{4}$ teaspoon	Hermesetas Liquid Sweetener	$\frac{1}{4}$ teaspoon
2 tablespoons	Marvel Yogurt (see page 98)	2 tablespoons

Mix the egg yolks with the vinegar, lemon juice, seasoning, mustard and Hermesetas. Whisk in the yogurt and refrigerate until needed.

Slimmers' Yogurt Dressing

See photograph on page 72
Makes 150 ml/¼ pint

Metric		Imperial
80	CALORIES	**80**
150 ml	**Marvel Yogurt (see page 98)**	¼ pint
½ teaspoon	**lemon juice**	½ teaspoon
1 tablespoon	**tomato purée**	1 tablespoon
6 drops	**Hermesetas Liquid Sweetener**	6 drops
1 tablespoon	**chopped basil, marjoram, parsley, tarragon or mint**	1 tablespoon
1 clove	**garlic, crushed**	1 clove
	salt and pepper	

Mix all the ingredients together, using the herb of your choice and adding garlic and seasoning according to taste.

Piquant Dressing

See photograph on page 74
Makes ¾ litre/1¼ pints

Metric		Imperial
525	CALORIES	**525**
600 ml	**made-up Marvel**	1 pint
1 tablespoon	**corn oil**	1 tablespoon
1	**egg**	1
150 ml	**white wine vinegar**	¼ pint
25 g	**plain flour**	1 oz
2 teaspoons	**salt**	2 teaspoons
	freshly ground white pepper	
1 teaspoon	**prepared mustard**	1 teaspoon
½ teaspoon	**Hermesetas Liquid Sweetener**	½ teaspoon

Pour the Marvel into a liquidiser with the oil, egg and vinegar. Blend together slowly, adding all the remaining ingredients except Hermesetas until smooth. Pour the mixture into a saucepan and heat, stirring continuously until boiling. Boil, still stirring for 3-4 minutes. Cool, add the Hermesetas then transfer to a container and cover. Keep for up to 3 weeks in the refrigerator.

Desserts

Many people who give advice about slimming suggest that desserts and puddings are entirely unnecessary, nutritionally, and should be cut out completely. But for many slimmers it is this advice which makes them give up their diets. Sweetness may be unnecessary to good health, but for some people it's very necessary for happiness. If you like sweetness it's better to eat puddings – and find those with the fewest calories.

The main ingredient contributing to the energy content of puddings is often sugar. So simply changing from sugar to a very low-calorie sweetener like Hermesetas Liquid Sweetener will cut calories dramatically.

This will work in recipes where sugar is used only as a sweetening agent and in a fluid form – like stewed fruit. However, remember to add the sweetener after boiling. But it won't work in recipes like sponge cakes where the sugar contributes to the physical structure of the food. Use Hermesetas Sprinkle Sweet Sweetener in such cases but follow the cooking hints obtainable from the manufacturer.

Fruits are inherently low calorie, and some are sweet. By mixing different fruits together, cooking them with unusual flavours or just cooking fruits you normally eat raw, you can get a host of interesting puddings. Try Baked Ginger Pears or Malvern Pudding and see what we mean.

Perhaps the nicest surprise of all is the variety of ice creams and sorbets you can make using fruits and Hermesetas Liquid Sweetener. A portion of Coffee Sorbet has 60 Calories, Italian-style Ice Cream 35 Calories and Raspberry and Redcurrant Mousse 60 Calories. By using Low Calorie Topping made from Marvel and lemon juice instead of cream or custard, you have all the low calorie desserts you'll want, even for special occasions when Fiesta Pancakes, Princess Pudding or Lemon Mousse will please everyone.

Fiesta Pancakes

See photograph on page 84
Serves 6

Metric		Imperial
930 (155)	CALORIES	**990 (165)**
	Batter	
100 g	**plain flour**	4 oz
	pinch of salt	
1	**egg**	1
300 ml	**made-up Marvel**	$\frac{1}{2}$ pint
	Filling	
225 g	**cooking apples, peeled, cored and sliced**	8 oz
225 g	**apricots, halved and stoned**	8 oz
50 g	**raisins**	2 oz
	pinch of grated nutmeg	
150 ml	**dry cider**	$\frac{1}{4}$ pint
$\frac{1}{2}$ teaspoon	**Hermesetas Liquid Sweetener**	$\frac{1}{2}$ teaspoon

First prepare the batter. Sift the flour into a bowl with the salt and make a well in the centre. Break the egg into the well and draw in the flour from the edges of the well using a wooden spoon. Gradually stir in the Marvel. Beat the batter until smooth and leave to stand for approximately 1 hour.

For the filling, mix the apple, apricots, raisins, nutmeg and cider in an ovenproof dish. Cover and cook in a moderate oven (160°C, 325°F, Gas Mark 3) for 50-60 minutes. When cooked, sweeten to taste with Hermesetas. Alternatively the fruit mixture may be cooked in a saucepan over a gentle heat. Remove a few pieces of fruit for decoration.

Lightly grease an 18-cm/7-inch non-stick frying pan. When hot, pour in a little batter, tilting the pan to give a thin even layer. When the pancake is set and lightly browned underneath toss or turn over to cook the other side. Layer the pancakes with greaseproof or absorbent kitchen paper as you cook them – this mixture should make 12 pancakes. If liked the pancakes can be frozen at this stage.

Place a spoonful of the compote fruit filling on each pancake and roll or fold. Serve hot with natural yogurt.

Alternatively decorate the pancakes with the reserved fruit before serving.

Baked Ginger Pears

See photograph opposite
Serves 4

Metric		Imperial
300 (75)	CALORIES	**300 (75)**
150 ml	water	$\frac{1}{4}$ pint
1 tablespoon	lemon juice	1 tablespoon
	few strips lemon rind	
$\frac{1}{2}$ teaspoon	ground ginger	$\frac{1}{2}$ teaspoon
$\frac{1}{2}$ teaspoon	Hermesetas Liquid Sweetener	$\frac{1}{2}$ teaspoon
4	firm pears	4
	Decoration	
	few toasted flaked almonds (optional)	

Put the water, lemon juice and rind in a saucepan and bring to the boil. Simmer for 2 minutes. Remove the pan from the heat and add the ginger and Hermesetas.

Peel the pears but leave whole with the stalks on. Place them in an ovenproof dish and pour over the liquid immediately to prevent discoloration. Cover with foil and cook in a moderate oven (180°C, 350°F, Gas Mark 4) for 50-60 minutes, basting frequently with the liquid. Decorate with the flaked almonds if used and serve hot or cold.

For a special occasion, omit the ginger and substitute dry white wine for the water.

Low-calorie Topping

See photograph opposite
Makes 150 ml/$\frac{1}{4}$ pint

Metric		Imperial
200	CALORIES	**200**
50 g	dry Marvel	2 oz
2 teaspoons	lemon juice	2 teaspoons
	few drops Hermesetas Liquid Sweetener	
	few drops vanilla essence (optional)	

Make the Marvel up to 150 ml/$\frac{1}{4}$ pint with iced water and stir in the lemon juice, Hermesetas and vanilla to taste (if used). Whisk hard with a rotary or electric whisk until very frothy and doubled in volume. The topping should hold the trail of the whisk. Make the topping up to 30 minutes before it is required.

Baked Ginger Pears (see above); Gooseberry Nutty Crumble (see page 88); Low-calorie Topping (see above)

Malvern Pudding

Serves 6

Metric		Imperial
420 (70)	CALORIES	**420 (70)**
450 g	**cooking apples, peeled, cored and sliced**	1 lb
1 teaspoon	**ground cinnamon**	1 teaspoon
1 teaspoon	**ground mixed spice**	1 teaspoon
	few drops Hermesetas Liquid Sweetener	
1 tablespoon	**custard powder**	1 tablespoon
300 ml	**made-up Marvel**	½ pint
25 g	**cornflakes**	1 oz
15 g	**hazelnuts, finely chopped**	½ oz

Place the apple in a saucepan and add a little water with half the cinnamon and mixed spice. Cook gently until the apple is soft, sweeten with Hermesetas and divide the mixture between six individual ramekin dishes.

Mix the custard powder with a little of the Marvel. When smooth, stir in the rest and bring to the boil slowly, stirring continuously. Add Hermesetas Liquid Sweetener to taste and pour the custard over the apple.

Lightly crush the cornflakes and mix with the remaining cinnamon, mixed spice and the hazelnuts. Sprinkle the mixture over the ramekins and place under a hot grill for a few minutes until golden brown on top.

Rhubarb and Ginger Crisp

Serves 4

Metric		Imperial
260 (65)	CALORIES	**260 (65)**
450 g	**rhubarb**	1 lb
	Hermesetas Liquid Sweetener to taste	
4	**slices Slimcea**	4
½ teaspoon	**ground ginger**	½ teaspoon
25 g	**Outline**	1 oz

Slice the rhubarb into 2.5-cm/1-inch lengths and cook in a little water until just tender, about 5 minutes. Add Hermesetas to taste. Transfer to an ovenproof dish and keep hot.

Make the Slimcea into breadcrumbs and mix with the ginger. Melt the Outline in a frying pan and fry the crumbs in it until golden. Scatter the crumbs over the rhubarb and serve immediately.

Princess Pudding (see page 89); Fiesta Pancakes (see page 81)

Sweet Soufflé Omelette with Fruit Filling

Serves 4

Metric		Imperial
560 (140)	CALORIES	**560 (140)**
4	**eggs, separated**	4
2 tablespoons	**water**	2 tablespoons
$\frac{1}{4}$ teaspoon	**Hermesetas Liquid Sweetener**	$\frac{1}{4}$ teaspoon
2 drops	**vanilla essence**	2 drops
15 g	**Outline**	$\frac{1}{2}$ oz
	Filling	
2	**small bananas, mashed or**	2
100 g	**raspberries or strawberries crushed with a few drops of Hermesetas Liquid Sweetener**	4 oz

Mix the egg yolks with the water, Hermesetas and vanilla essence. Beat until thoroughly mixed. Whisk the egg whites until stiff then fold into the yolk mixture using a metal spoon. Heat the Outline in an omelette pan and allow to spread evenly. Pour in the egg mixture and cook without stirring on a low heat until well risen and golden brown underneath. Transfer to a pre-heated grill to brown the top. Mark a fold down the centre with a knife to make folding easy. Add the chosen filling and fold in two. Turn out and serve at once.

Banana Jamaica

See photograph on page 94
Serves 6

Metric		Imperial
960 (160)	CALORIES	**960 (160)**
6	**small bananas**	6
	juice of 1 lemon	
40 g	**Outline**	$1\frac{1}{2}$ oz
	few drops of Hermesetas Liquid Sweetener	
	juice of 2 oranges	
	pared rind of 1 orange	
	pinch of ground cinnamon	
3 tablespoons	**rum or cognac**	3 tablespoons
25 g	**almonds, roasted and chopped**	1 oz

Peel the bananas and brush with the lemon juice. Melt the Outline in a large frying pan and fry the bananas on both sides until golden brown. Arrange the bananas on a dish. Add the Hermesetas, remaining lemon and orange juice, half the pared orange rind, cinnamon and rum or cognac to the pan and bring to the boil. Cook for a few minutes then pour over the bananas, or if liked pour half the sauce over and serve the other half separately. Sprinkle the bananas with the almonds and remaining pared orange rind before serving.

Plum and Rhubarb Crunch

Serves 4

Metric		Imperial
580 (145)	CALORIES	**580 (145)**
4	**large ripe plums**	4
225 g	**rhubarb**	8 oz
4 tablespoons	**water**	4 tablespoons
1 teaspoon	**Hermesetas Liquid Sweetener**	1 teaspoon
7	**pieces rye crispbread**	7
$\frac{1}{4}$ teaspoon	**ground cinnamon**	$\frac{1}{4}$ teaspoon
	grated rind of 1 orange	
25 g	**Outline, melted**	1 oz
25 g	**hazelnuts, chopped and toasted**	1 oz
2 tablespoons	**Sprinkle Sweet Sweetener**	2 tablespoons
	Decoration	
	slices of orange	

Remove the stones from the plums and cut the rhubarb into 2.5-cm/1-inch lengths. Turn into a saucepan with the water and cook gently for 5 minutes or until the fruit is just tender. Sweeten with the Hermesetas and pour into an ovenproof dish.

　　Crush the crispbread and mix with the cinnamon, orange rind, Outline and hazelnuts. Stir in the Sprinkle Sweet and spoon the mixture over the fruit. Cook in a moderately hot oven (190°C, 375°F, Gas Mark 5) for 20 minutes until the topping is crisp. Decorate with orange slices.

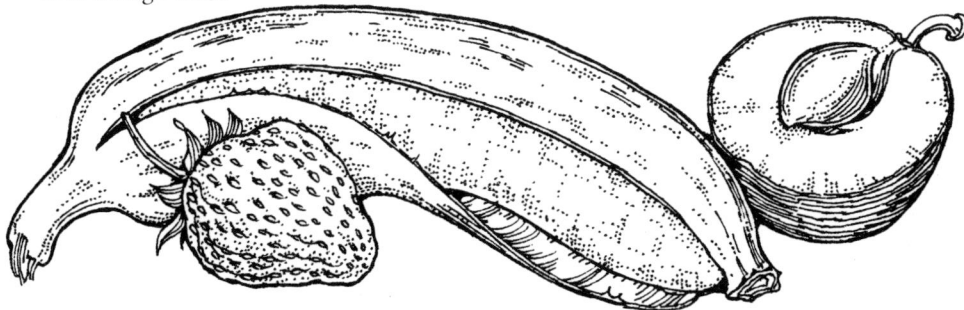

Eve's Temptation Apples

Serves 4

Metric		Imperial
560 (140)	CALORIES	**560 (140)**
2	**large cooking apples**	2
2 tablespoons	**water**	2 tablespoons
1 teaspoon	**lemon juice**	1 teaspoon
	Hermesetas Liquid Sweetener to taste	
5	**slices Slimcea**	5
50 g	**Outline**	2 oz
	grated rind of 1 large lemon	
2 teaspoons	**Sprinkle Sweet Sweetener**	2 teaspoons

Peel, core and slice the apples. Cook the apple with the water and lemon juice until the slices are just soft. Add liquid Hermesetas to taste.

Spread the Slimcea with most of the Outline, reserving a little for the topping. Cut the bread into fingers and use to line an ovenproof dish, Outline side down. Arrange the cooked apple in the middle and sprinkle the lemon rind and Sprinkle Sweet on top.

Dot with the remaining Outline and bake in a moderately hot oven (200°C, 400°F, Gas Mark 6) for 20 minutes.

Gooseberry Nutty Crumble

See photograph on page 83
Serves 4

Metric		Imperial
580 (145)	CALORIES	**580 (145)**
450 g	**gooseberries**	1 lb
6 tablespoons	**water**	6 tablespoons
	Hermesetas Liquid Sweetener to taste	
50 g	**plain flour**	2 oz
$\frac{1}{4}$ teaspoon	**ground cinnamon**	$\frac{1}{4}$ teaspoon
25 g	**Outline**	1 oz
25 g	**hazelnuts, chopped and toasted**	1 oz
1 tablespoon	**Sprinkle Sweet Sweetener**	1 tablespoon

Place the gooseberries in a saucepan with the water and cook until tender, about 5–10 minutes. Add Hermesetas to taste. Turn into a shallow ovenproof dish and set aside.

Sift the flour and cinnamon into a bowl, rub in the Outline and stir in the hazelnuts and Sprinkle Sweet. Spoon this mixture over the gooseberries. Bake in a moderately hot oven (190°C, 375°F, Gas Mark 5) for 30–40 minutes, until the topping is golden and crisp.

Princess Pudding

See photograph on page 84
Serves 4

Metric		Imperial
600 (150)	CALORIES	**600 (150)**
1½ tablespoons	**Slimcea breadcrumbs**	1½ tablespoons
15 g	**Outline**	½ oz
	Hermesetas Liquid Sweetener to taste	
450 ml	**made-up Marvel**	¾ pint
	grated rind of ½ lemon	
2	**eggs, separated**	2
	few drops vanilla essence	
2 tablespoons	**low-calorie jam**	2 tablespoons
3 tablespoons	**Sprinkle Sweet Sweetener**	3 tablespoons

Mix the Slimcea, Outline and Hermesetas together in a bowl. Heat the Marvel gently and pour it over the crumbs. Add the lemon rind, egg yolks and vanilla essence and pour into a 1-litre/1½-pint ovenproof dish. Bake in the centre of a moderate oven (180°C, 350°F, Gas Mark 4) for 30 minutes or until set. Reset the oven to hot (220°C, 425°F, Gas Mark 7).

Spread the jam over the top. Whisk the egg whites until stiff, then whisk in the Sprinkle Sweet until the egg whites are very dry. Pile or pipe on top of the pudding and brown in the hot oven for 3-5 minutes.

Italian-style Ice Cream

See photograph on page 93
Serves 6

Metric		Imperial
210 (35)	CALORIES	**210 (35)**
50 g	**dry Marvel**	2 oz
½ teaspoon	**Hermesetas Liquid Sweetener**	½ teaspoon
¼ teaspoon	**vanilla essence**	¼ teaspoon
1	**egg white**	1

Make the Marvel up to 150 ml/¼ pint with iced water. Stir in the Hermesetas and vanilla and whisk, using an electric whisk, until thick and frothy. Whisk the egg white until stiff and fold in using a metal spoon. Pour into a shallow container and freeze. This ice cream can be served with fruit purée sweetened with Hermesetas Liquid Sweetener.

Citron Champagne Sorbet

See photograph on page 93
Serves 2-3

Metric		Imperial
240 (120-80)	CALORIES	**240 (120-80)**
1 teaspoon	**powdered gelatine**	1 teaspoon
5 tablespoons	**lemon juice**	5 tablespoons
5 tablespoons	**Champagne**	5 tablespoons
5 tablespoons	**dry white wine**	5 tablespoons
2 teaspoons	**Hermesetas Liquid Sweetener**	2 teaspoons
	grated rind of ½ lemon and 1 orange	
1	**egg, separated**	1
	Decoration	
	pared orange and lemon rind	

Mix the gelatine with 2 tablespoons of the lemon juice in a small bowl. Stand this in a pan over hot water until dissolved. Mix the Champagne, wine, remaining lemon juice, Hermesetas and fruit rinds together. Stir in the dissolved gelatine.

Whisk the egg white until stiff, then add the egg yolk and continue to whisk until thoroughly mixed. Gradually whisk in the Champagne mixture. Pour into a container and leave in a freezer until half frozen. Turn out into a basin and whisk again. Return to the container and freeze again until firm. Soften slightly for 30 minutes in the refrigerator before serving in individual glasses. The sorbet may be served using a food baller. Decorate with the pared orange and lemon rinds.

Iced Coffee Sorbet

See photograph on page 93
Serves 4

Metric		Imperial
240 (60)	CALORIES	**240 (60)**
50 g	**dry Marvel**	2 oz
600 ml	**strong black coffee, chilled**	1 pint
1 teaspoon	**Hermesetas Liquid Sweetener**	1 teaspoon
2	**egg whites**	2
	Decoration	
	grated chocolate	

Make the Marvel up to 150 ml/¼ pint with some of the coffee. Whisk, using an electric whisk, until the mixture becomes thick and frothy. Gradually whisk in the remaining coffee and the Hermesetas. Pour into a shallow container and place in the freezer until half frozen. Whisk the mixture thoroughly and whisk the egg whites until stiff. Fold the egg white into the coffee mixture using a metal spoon and return the mixture to the freezer until firm. Serve in elegant glasses, topped with a little grated chocolate for a special occasion.

Apple Snow

See photograph on page 134
Serves 6

Metric		Imperial
510 (85)	CALORIES	**510 (85)**
450 g	**cooking apples**	1 lb
	few drops lemon juice	
	Hermesetas Liquid Sweetener to taste	
	few drops green food colouring (optional)	
300 ml	**made-up Marvel**	$\frac{1}{2}$ pint
1 teaspoon	**custard powder**	1 teaspoon
2	**eggs, separated**	2
2 teaspoons	**Hermesetas Liquid Sweetener**	2 teaspoons
	Decoration	
1	**dessert apple, sliced**	1

Core, but do not peel the apples. Slice the apples and cook in the lemon juice and a very little water until tender. Purée the apple and add Hermesetas to taste. If liked, add a few drops of green food colouring at this stage.

Mix a little of the Marvel with the custard powder and heat the rest in a saucepan. Mix the egg yolks with the custard powder and Hermesetas and stir in the heated Marvel. Stir well and return to the pan. Heat gently without boiling, stirring continuously until thickened. Cool the custard and mix with the purée. Chill. Whisk the egg whites until stiff and fold into the apple mixture. Divide the mixture between six glasses and decorate with slices of the dessert apple. Serve within an hour.

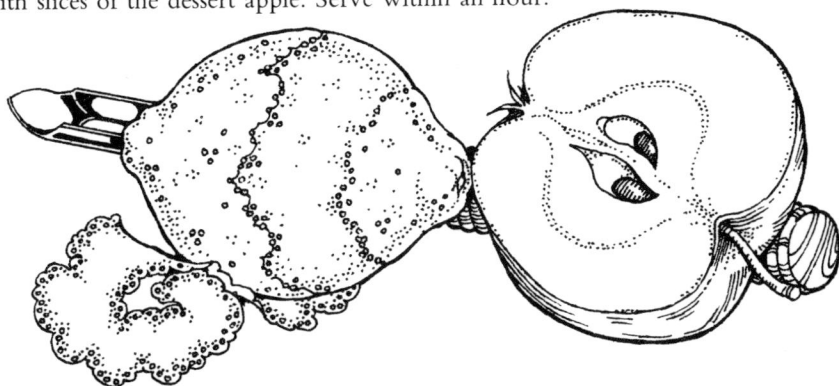

Apricot Sherbet

Serves 4

Metric		Imperial
360 (90)	CALORIES	**360 (90)**
50 g	dried apricots	2 oz
600 ml	water	1 pint
½ teaspoon	Hermesetas Liquid Sweetener	½ teaspoon
2 teaspoons	powdered gelatine	2 teaspoons
2 tablespoons	hot water	2 tablespoons
50 g	dry Marvel	2 oz
1	egg white	1

Soak the apricots in the water overnight, then simmer in the liquid for 30 minutes. Sieve or liquidise the apricots with the remaining liquid to make a smooth purée. Leave to cool completely then mix with the Hermesetas. Dissolve the gelatine in the hot water in a basin over a pan of hot water. Make the Marvel up to 150 ml/¼ pint with iced water. Whisk thoroughly, preferably using an electric whisk, until very frothy. Whisk in the gelatine and continue to whisk until the mixture forms a thick, pale cream. Whisk in the apricot purée. Whisk the egg white until stiff and fold into the mixture. Turn into a rigid freezer container and freeze until firm. Alternatively this may be divided between individual glasses and chilled thoroughly before serving.

Fruit Fool

Serves 4

Metric		Imperial
240 (60)	CALORIES	**240 (60)**
350 g	soft fruit	12 oz
	Hermesetas Liquid Sweetener to taste	
300 ml	Marvel Yogurt (see page 98)	½ pint

Reserve a little of the fruit for decoration. Cook the remainder with a little water until just soft. Reduce to a purée by sieving or liquidising; in the case of blackberries, blackcurrants or gooseberries sieve the purée from the liquidiser to remove any pips. Add Hermesetas to taste and stir well. Allow to cool. Whisk the yogurt lightly and mix with the purée. Pour into individual dishes and chill well before serving in individual glasses, decorated with some of the reserved fruit.

Iced Coffee Sorbet (see page 90); Italian-style Ice Cream (see page 89); Citron Champagne Sorbet (see page 90)

Chocolate Whip

Serves 6

Metric		Imperial
570 (95)	CALORIES	**570 (95)**
1 tablespoon	**powdered gelatine**	1 tablespoon
2 tablespoons	**hot water**	2 tablespoons
600 ml	**made-up Marvel**	1 pint
1 tablespoon	**cornflour**	1 tablespoon
1	**egg, separated**	1
2 tablespoons	**cocoa powder**	2 tablespoons
1 teaspoon	**vanilla essence**	1 teaspoon
$\frac{3}{4}$ teaspoon	**Hermesetas Liquid Sweetener**	$\frac{3}{4}$ teaspoon
25 g	**dry Marvel**	1 oz
150 ml	**ice cold water**	$\frac{1}{4}$ pint
	Decoration	
	grated chocolate (optional)	

Dissolve the gelatine in the hot water in a bowl over a pan of simmering water. Mix a little of the Marvel with the cornflour, egg yolk, cocoa powder and vanilla until smooth and creamy. Heat the remaining Marvel and gradually stir into the creamed mixture. Return to the pan and bring to the boil, stirring continuously. Remove from the heat and when slightly cooled add the gelatine. Leave to cool, stirring occasionally to prevent a skin forming. Add the Hermesetas and chill until the mixture begins to set.

Whisk the egg white with the dry Marvel and iced water until creamy. The mixture should hold the trail of the whisk. Fold this into the half set chocolate mixture and divide between six individual glasses. Chill until set. Sprinkle with a little grated chocolate, if liked.

Previous pages *Banana Jamaica (see page 86); Charlotte Russe (see page 107) Marvel Yogurt (see page 98)*

Marvel Yogurt

See photograph on page 96

There are several ways to make yogurt at home and it is well worth the effort if you use a fair amount. Start with a good quality commercially-produced natural yogurt. Several makes of electric yogurt-maker are available, so follow the instructions with each appliance.

When making yogurt in a flask, remember to sterilise all the equipment, otherwise the yogurt may be rather thin.

Makes 600 ml/1 pint

Metric		Imperial
375	CALORIES	375
600 ml	water	1 pint
8 heaped tablespoons	dry Marvel	8 heaped tablespoons
2 tablespoons	commercial natural yogurt	2 tablespoons

Boil the water and pour into a sterilised bowl. Cover and leave to stand for 2 hours. The ideal temperature is about 40°C/104°F. Sterilise a measuring spoon, whisk and vacuum flask and have them warm ready for use. Using the sterilised equipment, whisk the Marvel and yogurt into the water and pour into the warmed flask. Seal the flask and leave undisturbed overnight. Use the yogurt as required. Keep some of each batch to start the next one for convenience. Add fresh fruit if liked.

Rosy Apples

Serves 6

Metric		Imperial
780 (130)	CALORIES	780 (130)
675 g	cooking apples, peeled, cored and sliced	1½ lb
150 ml	blackcurrant cordial	¼ pint
15 g	powdered gelatine	½ oz
50 g	dry Marvel	2 oz
150 ml	Marvel Yogurt (see above)	¼ pint

Place the apples in a saucepan with the cordial and simmer until soft. Liquidise or sieve to make a smooth purée.

Mix the gelatine with 2 tablespoons water in a small bowl and stand over a pan of hot water until the gelatine is dissolved. Pour the gelatine into the purée in a steady stream, stirring thoroughly. Leave to cool.

Make up the Marvel to 300 ml/½ pint with water and stir into the cooling purée. As the mixture starts to set, spoon into glasses and swirl the yogurt on top. Chill thoroughly before serving.

Lemon Mousse

Serves 4

Metric		Imperial
540 (135)	CALORIES	**540 (135)**
15 g	**powdered gelatine**	$\frac{1}{2}$ oz
4 tablespoons	**water**	4 tablespoons
	grated rind and juice of 2 lemons	
3	**eggs, separated**	3
3 tablespoons	**Sprinkle Sweet Sweetener**	3 tablespoons
	Decoration	
	pared lemon rind	

Mix the gelatine and water in a small bowl and stand over a pan of hot water until the gelatine dissolves. Stir the lemon juice into the gelatine and allow to cool.

Mix the lemon rind with the egg yolks and Sprinkle Sweet in a bowl. Whisk the mixture until pale and creamy. Gradually beat in the gelatine mixture and leave until it begins to set. Whisk the egg whites until stiff and fold into the lemon mixture with a metal spoon. Pour into individual serving dishes and chill until set. Decorate with a little pared lemon rind.

Raspberry and Redcurrant Mousse

Serves 6

Metric		Imperial
300 (50)	CALORIES	**300 (50)**
175 g	**redcurrants**	6 oz
150 ml	**water**	$\frac{1}{4}$ pint
$\frac{3}{4}$ teaspoon	**Hermesetas Liquid Sweetener**	$\frac{3}{4}$ teaspoon
225 g	**raspberries**	8 oz
150 ml	**Marvel Yogurt (see page 98)**	$\frac{1}{4}$ pint
15 g	**powdered gelatine**	$\frac{1}{2}$ oz
2 tablespoons	**hot water**	2 tablespoons
2	**egg whites**	2

Poach the redcurrants in the water until soft. Liquidise and sieve the fruit to make a smooth purée without pips. Cool before adding the Hermesetas. Set aside one-quarter of the raspberries for decoration. Add the rest to the redcurrant purée with the yogurt. Mix the gelatine with the hot water in a small bowl and stand over a pan of hot water until the gelatine is dissolved. Stir briskly into the fruit mixture and leave until the mixture is beginning to set. Whisk the egg whites until stiff then fold into the fruit mixture. Pour into a mould and chill until set. Unmould and decorate with the reserved raspberries.

Fruit Cheese

Serves 6

Metric		Imperial
810 (135)	CALORIES	**810 (135)**
225 g	**soft fruit (blackcurrants, raspberries or gooseberries are particularly suitable)**	8 oz
2 tablespoons	**Sprinkle Sweet Sweetener (optional)**	2 tablespoons
225 g	**curd cheese**	8 oz
3	**eggs**	3
3 heaped tablespoons	**dry Marvel**	3 heaped tablespoons
1 teaspoon	**Hermesetas Liquid Sweetener**	1 teaspoon

Clean the fruit according to type and divide it between six individual ramekin dishes. Sprinkle with Sprinkle Sweet Sweetener if liked.

Soften the cheese a little and beat in the eggs. Mix the Marvel with 300 ml/$\frac{1}{2}$ pint cold water and mix it into the cheese with the Hermesetas. Divide the mixture between the ramekins, stand them in a baking dish of water so that the water comes halfway up the sides of the ramekin dishes, and cook in a moderate oven (180°C, 350°F, Gas Mark 4) for 30-40 minutes, until set. Chill before serving.

Slimmers' Cheesecake

Serves 6

Metric		Imperial
660 (110)	CALORIES	**660 (110)**
225 g	**cottage cheese, sieved**	8 oz
150 ml	**Marvel Yogurt (see page 98)**	$\frac{1}{4}$ pint
4 tablespoons	**low-calorie lemon squash**	4 tablespoons
	grated rind and juice of 1 lemon	
$\frac{3}{4}$ teaspoon	**Hermesetas Liquid Sweetener**	$\frac{3}{4}$ teaspoon
15 g	**powdered gelatine**	$\frac{1}{2}$ oz
2 tablespoons	**hot water**	2 tablespoons
2	**egg whites**	2
	Decoration	
50 g	**grapes**	2 oz
1	**lemon, thinly sliced**	1

Line a 15-cm/6-inch loose-bottomed cake tin with greaseproof paper. Mix together the cottage cheese, yogurt, lemon squash, lemon rind and juice. Sweeten with Hermesetas.

Mix the gelatine with the water in a small bowl and stand over a pan of hot water until the gelatine is dissolved. Stir the gelatine into the cheese mixture and leave until just setting. Whisk the egg whites until stiff and fold into the mixture with a metal spoon. Turn into the tin and chill until firm. Turn out and decorate with the grapes and lemon slices.

Gâteau Café

Serves 8

Metric		Imperial
1040 (130)	CALORIES	**1040 (130)**
4	**eggs, separated**	4
4 tablespoons	**Sprinkle Sweet Sweetener**	4 tablespoons
75 g	**plain flour**	3 oz
3 tablespoons	**strong black coffee**	3 tablespoons
	Filling	
50 g	**dry Marvel**	2 oz
1 teaspoon	**powdered gelatine**	1 teaspoon
1 tablespoon	**hot water**	1 tablespoon
1 teaspoon	**instant coffee powder**	1 teaspoon
$\frac{1}{2}$ teaspoon	**Hermesetas Liquid Sweetener**	$\frac{1}{2}$ teaspoon
	Decoration	
2 teaspoons	**grated chocolate**	2 teaspoons

Base-line two 20-cm/8-inch sandwich tins with greaseproof paper.

Whisk the egg yolks and Sprinkle Sweet Sweetener together until thick and creamy. Sift the flour and fold in with the coffee. Whisk the egg whites until stiff and fold into the yolk mixture. Divide this mixture evenly between the two sandwich tins and bake in a moderately hot oven (190°C, 375°F, Gas Mark 5) for 20-30 minutes. Peel off the greaseproof paper and cool on a wire rack. Sandwich the sponge layers together with the coffee filling.

To make the filling, make the Marvel up to 150 ml/$\frac{1}{4}$ pint with iced water. Dissolve the gelatine in the hot water in a basin over a pan of simmering water. Whisk the Marvel mixture, preferably using an electric whisk, until very frothy and thick. Dissolve the coffee in 2 teaspoons of boiling water, cool slightly then whisk into the Marvel together with the gelatine and Hermesetas. Continue whisking until very thick and creamy.

Sandwich the cake together with half the coffee cream and swirl the remainder over the top. Decorate with a little grated chocolate.

Seville Loaf

See photograph on page 106
Makes 1 loaf (10 slices)

Metric		Imperial
1200 (120)	CALORIES	**1200 (120)**
150 g	**self-raising flour**	5 oz
	pinch of salt	
3 tablespoons	**Sprinkle Sweet Sweetener**	3 tablespoons
75 g	**Outline**	3 oz
	grated rind of ½ orange	
2 tablespoons	**low-calorie marmalade**	2 tablespoons
3 tablespoons	**unsweetened orange juice**	3 tablespoons
2	**eggs, separated**	2
1 tablespoon	**low-calorie marmalade to glaze**	1 tablespoon

Place all the ingredients except the egg whites and glaze in a bowl and beat, preferably using an electric whisk, until thoroughly combined. Whisk the egg whites until soft and fold in with a metal spoon.

Pour into a greased 0.5-kg/1-lb loaf tin and bake in a moderate oven (180°C, 350°F, Gas Mark 4) for 50-60 minutes until golden. Cool on a wire rack. Warm the marmalade for the glaze and brush on while still hot.

Nutty Banana Teabread

See photograph on page 106
Makes 1 loaf (16 slices)

Metric		Imperial
1920 (120)	CALORIES	**1920 (120)**
50 g	**Outline**	2 oz
3	**medium bananas, mashed**	3
4 tablespoons	**Sprinkle Sweet Sweetener**	4 tablespoons
1	**egg, beaten**	1
	grated rind of 1 orange	
275 g	**self-raising flour**	10 oz
	pinch of salt	
50 g	**walnuts, chopped**	2 oz

Beat the Outline with the bananas and Sprinkle Sweet Sweetener until thoroughly combined and soft. Stir in the egg and orange rind. Sift the flour and salt into a bowl and stir in the walnuts. Make a well in the middle and pour in the banana mixture. Gradually beat in the dry ingredients until thoroughly combined.

Base-line a 1-kg/2-lb loaf tin with greaseproof paper. Grease the tin and turn the mixture into it, spreading the top evenly. Bake in a moderate oven (180°C, 350°F, Gas Mark 4) for 1-1¼ hours. Turn out and cool on a wire rack. Serve each slice spread with Outline.

Black Cherry Gâteau

See photograph on page 105
Serves 8

Metric		Imperial
1680 (210)	CALORIES	**1840 (230)**
	All-in-one chocolate sandwich cake	
175 g	**Outline**	6 oz
6 heaped tablespoons	**Sprinkle Sweet Sweetener**	6 heaped tablespoons
3	**eggs**	3
150 g	**self-raising flour**	5 oz
25 g	**cocoa powder**	1 oz
1½ teaspoons	**baking powder**	1½ teaspoons
	grated rind of 1 orange	
	Filling	
100 g	**curd cheese**	4 oz
2 tablespoons	**Marvel Yogurt (see page 98)**	2 tablespoons
	few drops Hermesetas Liquid Sweetener (optional)	
100 g	**black cherries**	4 oz
1 teaspoon	**icing sugar**	1 teaspoon

Place all the sandwich cake ingredients in a bowl and beat thoroughly until well combined and soft in consistency.

Base-line two 18-cm/7-inch sandwich tins with greaseproof paper and divide the mixture evenly between them. Bake in a moderate oven (160°C, 325°F, Gas Mark 3) for about 30-35 minutes. Turn out and cool on a wire tray.

Beat the curd cheese with the yogurt and Hermesetas (if used). Spread the cheese over one layer of cake. Reserve a few cherries for decoration. Stone the remaining cherries and arrange on the cheese mixture. Place the second sandwich cake on top and sift the icing sugar over the top. Decorate with the reserved cherries.

Mandarin Eclairs

See photograph opposite
Makes 6

Metric		Imperial
540 (90)	CALORIES	**540 (90)**
	Choux pastry	
4 tablespoons	**water**	4 tablespoons
25 g	**Outline**	1 oz
40 g	**plain flour, sifted**	1½ oz
	pinch of salt	
1	**egg**	1
	Filling	
1 (298-g) can	**mandarin segments in natural juice**	1 (10½-oz) can
1 teaspoon	**arrowroot**	1 teaspoon
	Hermesetas Liquid Sweetener to taste	
	icing sugar for dusting	

First prepare the éclairs. Heat the water and Outline together in a saucepan until the Outline has melted. Bring to the boil, take from the heat and add all the flour and salt at once, beating until the mixture forms a smooth ball and leaves the sides of the pan. Cool slightly. Beat the egg and add to the mixture a little at a time, beating continuously until smooth and glossy.

Grease a baking tray and fit a plain 1.5-cm/¾-inch nozzle into a piping bag. Use this to pipe six fingers of the mixture on to the baking tray. Cook in a moderately hot oven (200°C, 400°F, Gas Mark 6) for 10 minutes, then reduce the temperature to 190°C, 375°F, Gas Mark 5 for a further 20 minutes. Split each finger and cool on a wire rack.

To make the filling, drain off and reserve the juice from the mandarins. Mix 6 tablespoons of the juice with the arrowroot and cook, stirring continuously in a small saucepan until thick and clear. Add Hermesetas to taste. Stir in the drained mandarins and allow to cool. Use the mixture to fill the éclairs, return the tops and dust with sifted icing sugar.

Mandarin Eclairs (see above); Black Cherry Gâteau (see page 103)

Charlotte Russe

See photogaph on page 94
Serves 8

Metric		Imperial
1200 (150)	CALORIES	**1200 (150)**
	Sponge fingers	
3	**eggs, separated**	3
3 tablespoons	**Sprinkle Sweet Sweetener**	3 tablespoons
50 g	**plain flour**	2 oz
2 tablespoons	**hot water**	2 tablespoons
	Filling	
1 (227-g) can	**pineapple rings in natural juice**	1 (8-oz) can
25 g	**powdered gelatine**	1 oz
225 g	**cottage cheese**	8 oz
150 ml	**Marvel Yogurt (see page 98)**	$\frac{1}{4}$ pint
	grated rind of 1 lemon	
2 tablespoons	**Sprinkle Sweet Sweetener**	2 tablespoons
2	**eggs, separated**	2

First make the sponge fingers. Whisk the egg yolks with the Sprinkle Sweet Sweetener until pale and creamy. Sift the flour and fold into the egg yolks together with the hot water. Whisk the egg whites until stiff and fold into the yolk mixture using a metal spoon. Fit a piping bag with a 1.5-cm/$\frac{3}{4}$-inch plain nozzle and pipe 7.5-cm/3-inch lengths of the sponge mixture on greased baking trays. Bake in a moderate oven (180°C, 350°F, Gas Mark 4) for 10 minutes. Carefully remove the fingers from the baking trays and cool on a wire rack.

Drain the juice from the canned pineapple and make up to 300 ml/$\frac{1}{2}$ pint with cold water. Dissolve half the gelatine in 2 tablespoons of the juice mixture in a small basin over a pan of hot water. Mix the gelatine into the rest of the juice. Arrange some of the pineapple in the base of an 18-cm/7-inch Charlotte mould and spoon a little of the gelatine mixture over. Leave to set quickly in a refrigerator. Dip the sponge fingers in the gelatine mixture and line the sides of the mould with them. Leave to set. Allow the remaining gelatine mixture to set.

Liquidise the remaining pineapple with the cottage cheese, yogurt, lemon rind, Sprinkle Sweet Sweetener and egg yolks until smooth. Dissolve the remaining 15 g/$\frac{1}{2}$ oz gelatine in 3 tablespoons hot water and mix into the cottage cheese mixture. Leave until half set. Whisk the egg whites until stiff and fold in using a metal spoon. Turn into the lined mould and leave to set. To unmould the Charlotte russe, dip the tin in hot water for a few seconds then invert on to a serving dish. Chop the reserved jelly using a wet knife. Arrange this around the Charlotte Russe.

Nutty Banana Teabread (see page 102); Seville Loaf (see page 102)

Suppers, snacks and packed meals

If it's 10 pm, you've missed your proper evening meal and eaten only a light lunch, there's a great temptation to have something filling and quick. A cheese sandwich and a couple of chocolate biscuits seem ideal. But that modest snack could add up to a not-very-modest 550 Calories if you use ordinary bread and butter or margarine and a tiny 25 g/1 oz of Cheddar cheese.

If you do decide to have a late supper instead of an evening meal, or as well as afternoon tea, think hard about what you're going to eat. You'll find plenty of ideas in this section. Fish Soufflé, Mushroom Puffs, Courgette Exquise and Piperade with Eggs all give 250 to 300 Calories per portion.

More suitable for packed lunches are Egg Tartlets, Slimcea Sandwiches (spread with Outline) and Lemon Sardine Loaf. It isn't easy to think beyond ham sandwiches when you're packing your lunch at 7.30 am. But a little thought and imagination can work wonders. There are plenty of salads you can make up yourself. Try combinations of cucumber, rice, pasta shells, sweetcorn, peppers, raw cabbage, grated carrot, diced celery, with egg, chopped meats, cottage cheese, prawns and chopped chicken. Pack these in Outline tubs or cottage cheese tubs with well-fitting lids, but overwrap with polythene to be sure of avoiding spills.

For afternoon tea occasions when cream and well-buttered sandwiches can put paid to any slimming diet, try Slimcea Open Sandwiches and Piquant Pinwheels, with Seville Loaf (see page 102), Nutty Banana Teabread (see page 102) and Mandarin Eclairs (see page 104). You'll have food to entertain Royalty, and your neighbours!

Slimmers' Pastry

Makes 225 g/8 oz

Metric		Imperial
1160	CALORIES	**1220**
225 g	**plain flour**	8 oz
100 g	**Outline**	4 oz
1 tablespoon	**cold water**	1 tablespoon

Sift the flour into a bowl and rub in the Outline until the mixture resembles fine breadcrumbs. Gradually mix in the water to form a dough. Use as required.

Capsicum Tart

Serves 4

Metric		Imperial
1840 (460)	CALORIES	**1920 (480)**
225 g	**Slimmers' Pastry (see page 108)**	8 oz
25 g	**Outline**	1 oz
1	**onion, finely chopped**	1
1	**red pepper, seeds removed and sliced**	1
1	**green pepper, seeds removed and sliced**	1
3	**eggs**	3
300 ml	**made-up Marvel**	½ pint
1 tablespoon	**Slimcea breadcrumbs**	1 tablespoon
25 g	**cheese, grated**	1 oz
	salt and pepper	

Prepare the pastry according to the recipe instructions and use to line a 23-cm/9-inch flan ring. Bake blind in a moderately hot oven (200°C, 400°F, Gas Mark 6) for 15 minutes. Heat the Outline in a frying pan and cook the onion and peppers until soft. Beat the eggs with the Marvel and breadcrumbs, add the cheese and season to taste. Arrange the pepper and onion mixture in the flan case and pour the egg mixture over. Bake in a moderate oven (180°C, 350°F, Gas Mark 4) for 40-45 minutes until golden brown and set.

Cheese and Apple Hot Pot

Serves 4

Metric		Imperial
1560 (390)	CALORIES	**1560 (390)**
450 g	**cooking apples**	1 lb
	salt and pepper	
3 tablespoons	**Slimcea breadcrumbs**	3 tablespoons
200 g	**cheese, grated**	7 oz
3	**eggs**	3
300 ml	**made-up Marvel**	½ pint

Peel and core the apples and cut into thick slices. Put a layer of apple in the bottom of a greased ovenproof dish. Season the breadcrumbs and sprinkle a layer over the apple. Cover with a layer of cheese and continue until the apple, breadcrumbs and cheese are used up, ending with a cheese layer. Beat the eggs, season well and stir in the Marvel. Strain over the cheese mixture then bake in a moderate oven (180°C, 350°F, Gas Mark 4) for 50-60 minutes, or until set and browned on top.

Cheese Pie

Serves 4

Metric		Imperial
1200 (300)	CALORIES	**1200 (300)**
6	slices Slimcea	6
2	eggs	2
1	onion, finely chopped	1
175 g	Cheddar cheese, grated	6 oz
2	slices ham, chopped	2
	salt and pepper	

Lightly grease an ovenproof dish and line it with the Slimcea. Beat the eggs and add the onion, 150 g/5 oz of the cheese, the ham and seasoning to taste. Pour the mixture into the lined dish and stand for 30 minutes. Sprinkle with the remaining cheese and cook in a moderate oven (180°C, 350°F, Gas Mark 4) for 40-45 minutes or until set and golden. Serve hot with a crisp salad.

Pipérade with Eggs

See photograph on page 136
Serves 4

Metric		Imperial
1080 (270)	CALORIES	**1080 (270)**
75 g	Outline	3 oz
1	large onion, sliced	1
1	green pepper, seeds removed and sliced	1
4	tomatoes, peeled and sliced	4
1 teaspoon	dried thyme	1 teaspoon
	salt and pepper	
4	eggs	4
	Garnish	
1 tablespoon	oil	1 tablespoon
4	slices Slimcea	4
1 tablespoon	chopped parsley	1 tablespoon

Melt two-thirds of the Outline in a deep frying pan. Add the onion, pepper, tomatoes, thyme and seasoning to taste. Stir thoroughly then cover and cook gently for 10 minutes or until soft.

Make four hollows in the mixture, using the back of a spoon, and break an egg into each. Cover and cook gently until the eggs are set.

110

Heat the remaining Outline with the oil in a shallow frying pan. Cut each slice of Slimcea into four triangles. Fry the croûtes until golden on both sides and sprinkle with seasoning. Use as a garnish together with the chopped parsley when serving the pipérade.

Courgette Exquise

Serves 4

Metric		Imperial
1100 (275)	CALORIES	**1100 (275)**
50 g	**Outline**	2 oz
675 g	**courgettes**	1½ lb
50 g	**Edam cheese, grated**	2 oz
100 g	**cooked chicken meat, diced**	4 oz
100 g	**ham, chopped**	4 oz
	All-in-one sauce	
25 g	**Outline**	1 oz
25 g	**flour**	1 oz
300 ml	**made-up Marvel**	½ pint
	salt and pepper	
1 tablespoon	**sherry**	1 tablespoon

Melt the Outline in a pan. Slice the courgettes diagonally and add to the Outline. Cook, stirring continuously, until they are tender. Transfer to an ovenproof dish. Sprinkle with a little of the cheese and arrange the chicken and ham over the top. Keep hot.

Place all the sauce ingredients except the sherry in a saucepan and bring to the boil, whisking continuously. Boil for 2-3 minutes. Remove from the heat and stir in the sherry. Pour over the courgettes and meats and top with the remaining cheese. Toast under a hot grill until golden. Serve with a green salad.

All-in-one Coating Sauce

Makes 150 ml/¼ pint

Metric		Imperial
160	CALORIES	**160**
150 ml	**made-up Marvel**	¼ pint
15 g	**Outline**	½ oz
1 tablespoon	**plain flour**	1 tablespoon

Place the Marvel and Outline in a small non-stick saucepan. Whisk in the flour. Cook over a gentle heat, whisking until the mixture boils. Cook for a further 2 minutes.

Mushroom Puff

Serves 4

Metric		Imperial
920 (230)	CALORIES	**920 (230)**
225 g	**button mushrooms**	8 oz
50 g	**Outline**	2 oz
1 clove	**garlic, crushed**	1 clove
	salt and pepper	
100 g	**cottage cheese, sieved**	4 oz
3	**eggs, separated**	3
8	**slices Slimcea, toasted**	8

Clean and quarter the mushrooms. Melt the Outline in a pan, add the garlic and mushrooms and season generously. Cook gently for a few minutes.

Mix the cottage cheese with the egg yolks and season to taste. Whisk the egg whites until stiff and fold into the yolk mixture. Divide the mushrooms between the toasted Slimcea and top each one with some of the egg mixture. Place under a preheated grill until slightly puffed and golden brown. Serve immediately.

Egg Tartlets

See photograph on page 136
Serves 4

Metric		Imperial
960 (240)	CALORIES	**960 (240)**
8	**slices Slimcea, crusts removed**	8
15 g	**Outline**	$\frac{1}{2}$ oz
	Filling	
1 quantity	**Slimmers' Mayonnaise (see page 78)**	1 quantity
1 clove	**garlic, crushed**	1 clove
2 tablespoons	**chopped parsley**	2 tablespoons
4	**hard-boiled eggs, finely chopped**	4
	Garnish	
1	**hard-boiled egg, halved and sliced**	1
	few sprigs parsley	

Use a rolling pin to roll the Slimcea out as thinly as possible. Spread both sides with the Outline and press into patty tins. Bake these in a moderately hot oven (200°C, 400°F, Gas Mark 6) for 10-15 minutes or until golden. Leave to cool while preparing the filling.

Mix together the Slimmers' Mayonnaise, garlic, parsley and eggs. Divide the mixture between the cases and chill. Garnish with halved egg slices and parsley before serving.

Fish Soufflé

Serves 4

Metric		Imperial
1000 (250)	CALORIES	**1000 (250)**
400 g	cooked white fish, flaked	14 oz
1 tablespoon	grated onion	1 tablespoon
2	eggs, separated	2
1 tablespoon	chopped parsley	1 tablespoon
4 tablespoons	Slimcea breadcrumbs	4 tablespoons
300 ml	hot made-up Marvel	½ pint
	salt and pepper	

Mix together the fish, onion, egg yolks, parsley and breadcrumbs. Gradually stir in the Marvel and seasoning. Whisk the egg whites until stiff and fold into the fish mixture. Turn into an ovenproof dish and stand in a baking dish of water so that the water comes halfway up the sides of the ovenproof dish. Cook in a moderate oven (180°C, 350°F, Gas Mark 4) for 40-45 minutes or until set and browned on top.

Tuna and Cheese Casserole

Serves 3

Metric		Imperial
1020 (340)	CALORIES	**1020 (340)**
1 (198-g) can	tuna, drained and flaked	1 (7-oz) can
2	eggs, beaten	2
225 g	cottage cheese	8 oz
6 tablespoons	Slimcea breadcrumbs	6 tablespoons
	salt and pepper	
	few drops Tabasco sauce	

Mix together the tuna, eggs, cottage cheese and half the breadcrumbs. Add seasoning and Tabasco to taste. Turn the mixture into a greased casserole dish and cover with the remaining breadcrumbs. Cook in a moderately hot oven (190°C, 375°F, Gas Mark 5) for 45-50 minutes until set and browned on top.

Lemon Sardine Loaf

Serves 8

Metric		Imperial
1280 (160)	CALORIES	**1280 (160)**
1 (120-g) can	**sardines in oil**	1 (4¼-oz) can
	salt and pepper	
	grated rind of 1 lemon	
2 teaspoons	**lemon juice**	2 teaspoons
1	**small clove garlic (optional)**	1
75 g	**Outline**	3 oz
1	**sliced Slimcea loaf**	1

Drain the sardines and mash thoroughly. Season and mix in the lemon rind, juice and garlic (if used). Beat in the Outline until pale and thoroughly combined. Spread the fish mixture on one side of each slice of the Slimcea loaf and pack the slices back together to re-form the loaf.

Wrap in foil and bake in a moderately hot oven (200°C, 400°F, Gas Mark 6) for 15-20 minutes, until the crusts are crisp. Serve immediately.

Note: *The loaf may be frozen with the fish mixture spread on each slice ready for heating through when required.*

Golden Cauliflower Toast

Serves 2

Metric		Imperial
400 (200)	CALORIES	**400 (200)**
½	**small cauliflower**	½
2	**rashers lean bacon**	2
1 tablespoon	**chopped chives**	1 tablespoon
2	**slices Slimcea, toasted**	2
	mustard for spreading	
25 g	**Cheddar cheese, grated**	1 oz

Cook the cauliflower in boiling salted water until just tender. Meanwhile grill the bacon until crisp, chop and mix with the chives. Spread the Slimcea toast with mustard. Break the cauliflower into florets and pile neatly on the toast. Sprinkle the grated cheese over the cauliflower and toast under a hot grill until the cheese is bubbling and melted. Sprinkle with the chopped bacon mixture.

Welsh Rarebit

Serves 2

Metric		Imperial
600 (300)	CALORIES	**600 (300)**
	knob of Outline	
2 heaped tablespoons	**dry Marvel**	2 heaped tablespoons
100 g	**Edam cheese, grated**	4 oz
	salt and pepper	
	pinch of dry mustard	
1 teaspoon	**capers**	1 teaspoon
4	**slices Slimcea, toasted**	4

Melt the Outline in a saucepan with 2 tablespoons water and the Marvel. Remove from the heat and add the cheese, seasoning, mustard and capers. Beat together until well mixed. Spread the mixture over the toasted Slimcea and grill until golden brown and bubbling.

Quickie Pizza

Serves 2

Metric		Imperial
400 (200)	CALORIES	**400 (200)**
2	**slices Slimcea**	2
½ teaspoon	**prepared mustard**	½ teaspoon
2	**tomatoes, peeled and sliced**	2
	salt and pepper	
½ teaspoon	**dried mixed herbs**	½ teaspoon
2	**slices Cheddar cheese**	2
2	**canned anchovy fillets**	2
4	**stuffed olives, halved**	4

Toast one side of the Slimcea and spread the untoasted side of each piece with mustard. Cover each slice with tomato, season, sprinkle with herbs and cover with a slice of cheese. Cut the anchovy fillets in half lengthways and arrange on the cheese. Toast under a hot grill until the cheese melts. Top each with the olives and serve at once.

Slimcea Sandwiches

See photograph on page 133
Serves 1

Metric		Imperial
2	**slices Slimcea**	2
15 g	**Outline for spreading**	$\frac{1}{2}$ oz
	One of the following fillings	

25 g/1 oz cottage cheese topped with 1 sliced peach. CALORIES Metric and Imperial **135**

50 g/2 oz flaked canned salmon or smoked salmon topped with snipped mustard and cress or lemon slices. CALOIES Metric and Imperial **200**

50 g/2 oz chopped crispy grilled lean bacon served on a bed of lettuce. CALORIES Metric and Imperial **270**

50 g/2 oz flaked canned tuna topped with 2 sliced tomatoes. CALORIES Metric and Imperial **260**

25 g/1 oz rolled lean roast beef topped with 6 sliced radishes. CALORIES Metric and Imperial **170**

25 g/1 oz rolled lean ham topped with 15 g/$\frac{1}{2}$ oz pickle and a few slices of cucumber. CALORIES Metric and Imperial **180**

1 sliced hard-boiled egg topped with a large sliced dill pickle. CALORIES Metric and Imperial **230**

50 g/2 oz cottage cheese combined with 1 teaspoon curry paste and topped with sliced cucumber. CALORIES Metric and Imperial **190**

50 g/2 oz grilled flaked kipper fillet seasoned with lemon juice to taste. CALORIES Metric and Imperial **225**

Spread the Slimcea with the Outline and fill with any of the above fillings. (If liked serve the sandwiches 'open', placing half the filling on each Slimcea slice.)

Garlic Bread

Serves 4

Metric		Imperial
560 (140)	CALORIES	**560 (140)**
50 g	**Outline**	2 oz
1	**large clove garlic, crushed**	1
	salt and pepper	
$\frac{1}{2}$	**sliced Slimcea loaf**	$\frac{1}{2}$

Beat the Outline, garlic and seasoning together and spread on one side of each slice of bread. Press the loaf back together and spread any remaining Outline mixture over the top. Wrap in foil and place in a moderately hot oven (200°C, 400°F, Gas Mark 6) for 15-20 minutes or until the Outline has melted into the bread and the crust is crisp. Serve hot from the oven.

Herb Bread

See photograph on page 30
Serves 4

Metric		Imperial
560 (140)	CALORIES	**560 (140)**
50 g	**Outline**	2 oz
2 tablespoons	**chopped mixed fresh herbs**	2 tablespoons
	(parsley, thyme, chives, rosemary)	
	salt and pepper	
$\frac{1}{2}$	**Slimcea loaf, sliced**	$\frac{1}{2}$

Method as garlic bread – substitute herbs for garlic.

Piquant Pinwheels

Serves 4

Metric		Imperial
880 (220)	CALORIES	**880 (220)**
$\frac{1}{2}$	**uncut Slimcea loaf**	$\frac{1}{2}$
40 g	**Outline for spreading**	$1\frac{1}{2}$ oz
225 g	**cottage cheese**	8 oz
1 quantity	**Slimmers' Mayonnaise (see page 78)**	1 quantity
1 teaspoon	**chopped parsley**	1 teaspoon
	grated rind of $\frac{1}{2}$ lemon	
1 teaspoon	**finely grated onion**	1 teaspoon
	salt and pepper	

Slice the loaf thinly lengthways and remove the crusts. Spread each slice with Outline. Prepare the filling by mixing all the other ingredients together. Spread this filling on each slice. Roll up the slices like individual Swiss rolls. Wrap and chill until firm. Cut in slices to serve.

Slimcea Open Sandwiches

See photograph on page 133
Serves 1

Metric		Imperial
2	**slices Slimcea**	2
	One of the following spreads and toppings	

Metric	*Italian*	Imperial
120	CALORIES	**120**
	few drops of anchovy essence for spreading	
25 g	**lean ham, chopped**	1 oz
1 teaspoon	**chopped onion**	1 teaspoon
2 teaspoons	**tomato purée**	2 teaspoons
	garlic salt	

Metric	*French*	Imperial
175	CALORIES	**175**
15 g	**Outline for spreading**	$\frac{1}{2}$ oz
25 g	**cooked chicken meat, chopped**	1 oz
1 tablespoon	**unsweetened apple sauce or purée**	1 tablespoon
1 teaspoon	**chopped parsley**	1 teaspoon
	sliced cucumber	

Metric	*Spanish*	Imperial
290	CALORIES	**290**
15 g	**Outline for spreading**	$\frac{1}{2}$ oz
25 g	**peeled prawns**	1 oz
25 g	**drained canned tuna, flaked**	1 oz
1	**tomato, peeled and chopped**	1
$\frac{1}{2}$	**hard-boiled egg, chopped**	$\frac{1}{2}$

Metric	*German*	Imperial
210	CALORIES	**210**
1 teaspoon	**German mustard for spreading**	1 teaspoon
1	**frankfurter, sliced**	1
25 g	**white cabbage, finely shredded**	1 oz
	Garnish	
	sprigs of watercress	

Spread the Slimcea according to the individual recipes. Top the Slimcea with the remaining ingredients. Serve two Slimcea Open Sandwiches per person.

Summertime Picnic Loaf

Serves 4

Metric		Imperial
960 (240)	CALORIES	**960 (240)**
$\frac{1}{2}$	**uncut Slimcea loaf**	$\frac{1}{2}$
75 g	**Outline**	3 oz
	First Filling	
50 g	**cottage cheese**	2 oz
$1\frac{1}{2}$	**sticks celery, finely chopped**	$1\frac{1}{2}$
	paprika	
	Second filling	
25 g	**Edam cheese, grated**	1 oz
2 teaspoons	**Slimmers' Mayonnaise (see page 78)**	2 teaspoons
$\frac{1}{4}$ bunch	**watercress, finely chopped**	$\frac{1}{4}$ bunch
	Third filling	
50 g	**cucumber, finely diced**	2 oz
40 g	**crabmeat**	$1\frac{1}{2}$ oz
1 tablespoon	**Slimmers' Mayonaise (see page 78)**	1 tablespoon
$\frac{1}{2}$ teaspoon	**grated lemon rind**	$\frac{1}{2}$ teaspoon
	salt and pepper	
1 teaspoon	**chopped parsley**	1 teaspoon
	Garnish	
	mustard and cress	

Slice the loaf horizontally into seven slices. Spread each one with Outline. Prepare the fillings by mixing each group of ingredients together. Sandwich the loaf back together, alternating the fillings to vary the colours. Spread the top with the remaining Outline and sprinkle with a line of mustard and cress.

Drinks

There are many low calorie fruit drinks on the market, and low calorie mixers for alcoholic drinks. When you realise that ordinary tonic can double the calorie value of a gin, you see how useful they can be. But there are occasions when orange squash and alcohol are not suitable. On hot summer days, for example, the last thing most people want is a stiff whisky or cup of tea. Water would satisfy your physiological needs, but not your taste buds. Sugary lemonade is out too. Most of the drinks in this section – both alcoholic and soft – contain only about 50 to 70 Calories a portion, and with plenty of ice they'll last a long time.

When you're entertaining a lot of people to cocktails it's amazing how much alcohol your guests can get through in an hour or so. These days, when more people are slimming, when more use cars and are conscious of drinking and driving, and when most of us are trying to economise a little, it makes a great deal of sense to offer two or three punches, at least one of which is non-alcoholic. Try Midsummer Punch, Iced Citrus or Apple, Ginger and Lime Cup for hot summer days; and Mulled Wine Cup or Normana Punch for cold winter evenings.

On the subject of cocktail parties do remember to offer some low calorie nibbles. A handful of peanuts may seem insignificant but its 150 Calories aren't. Try cruditées – thin strips of celery and carrot, slices of radish and cucumber crisped in cold water. Prunes with a flavoured cottage cheese stuffing are good too.

Tea and Orange Cooler

See photograph on page 123
Serves 4

Metric		Imperial
160 (40)	CALORIES	**160 (40)**
900 ml	**freshly-made fairly weak tea**	1½ pints
	pared rind of 1 orange	
150 ml	**unsweetened orange juice**	¼ pint
	juice of 1 lemon	
½ teaspoon	**Hermesetas Liquid Sweetener**	½ teaspoon
	Decoration	
2	**oranges, sliced**	2

Mix the tea and orange rind and leave to infuse until cold. Strain well and stir in the orange and lemon juices. Add Hermesetas to taste. Pour into a large jug and chill. Float orange slices on top before serving.

Apple, Ginger and Lime Cup

See photograph on page 123
Serves 2

Metric		Imperial
120 (60)	CALORIES	**120 (60)**
150 ml	**unsweetened apple juice**	¼ pint
	juice of 1 lime	
2 tablespoons	**ginger wine**	2 tablespoons
¼–½ teaspoon	**Hermesetas Liquid Sweetener**	¼–½ teaspoon
	soda water	
	ice cubes	
	Decoration	
2	**slices of lime**	2

Mix the apple juice, lime juice, ginger wine and Hermesetas together. Divide the mixture between two tall glasses and top up with soda water. Float ice cubes on top and decorate with slices of lime.

Pineapple Quencher

Serves 6

Metric		Imperial
720 (120)	CALORIES	**720 (120)**
450 ml	**Marvel Yogurt (see page 98)**	$\frac{3}{4}$ pint
600 ml	**unsweetened pineapple juice**	1 pint
	Hermesetas Liquid Sweetener to taste	
1 tablespoon	**lemon juice**	1 tablespoon
2-3 drops	**yellow food colouring**	2-3 drops
2 tablespoons	**Sprinkle Sweet Sweetener**	2 tablespoons

Mix the first three ingredients together and chill well. Take four fairly slim, tall wine glasses. Mix the lemon juice with a little food colouring in a small shallow dish. Spread the Sprinkle Sweet Sweetener out thinly on a piece of greaseproof paper. Dip the rim of the glasses in the lemon juice, allow any excess to drop off then dip in the Sprinkle Sweet Sweetener to give a yellow frosted rim. Fill each glass with the chilled pineapple drink.

Slimmers' Shake

See photograph on page 123
Serves 2

Metric		Imperial
140 (70)	CALORIES	**140 (70)**
25 g	**dry Marvel**	1 oz
300 ml	**water**	$\frac{1}{2}$ pint
100 g	**fresh fruit, skin and pips removed**	4 oz
	Hermesetas Liquid Sweetener to taste	
3	**ice cubes**	3
	Decoration	
	few pieces fresh fruit (optional)	

Put all the ingredients in a liquidiser and blend until smooth. Decorate with a few pieces of fruit if used and serve ice cold.

This drink may be served with a little Italian-style ice cream (see page 89) floated on top.

Apple, Ginger and Lime Cup (see page 121); Tea and Orange Cooler (see page 121); Slimmers' Shake (see above)

Iced Citrus

Serves 4

Metric		Imperial
280 (70)	CALORIES	**280 (70)**
4	**large oranges**	4
2	**large lemons**	2
600 ml	**boiling water**	1 pint
	Hermesetas Liquid Sweetener to taste	
	Decoration	
	slices of orange or lemon	

Pare the rind from 2 oranges and 1 lemon. Infuse the rind in the boiling water then leave until cold. Pour into the liquidiser with the squeezed juice from all the fruit. Liquidise, strain and sweeten to taste. Chill well before serving. Decorate the glasses with slices of orange or lemon.

Midsummer Punch

Serves 4

Metric		Imperial
240 (60)	CALORIES	**240 (60)**
300 ml	**unsweetened orange juice**	½ pint
300 ml	**unsweetened grapefruit juice**	½ pint
	juice of 2 lemons	
600 ml	**water**	1 pint
	Hermesetas Liquid Sweetener to taste	
	Decoration	
	slices of orange	

Mix all the ingredients together, pour into a large container and chill well before serving. Float orange slices in the punch.

Irish Coffee (see page 127); Mulled Wine Cup (see page 127)

Normana Punch

Serves 4

Metric		Imperial
480 (120)	CALORIES	**480 (120)**
1 bottle	**dry red wine**	1 bottle
	pared rind of 1 lemon and 1 orange	
1	**stick cinnamon**	1
	Hermesetas Liquid Sweetener to taste	
	Decoration	
	slices of orange	

Heat the wine with the lemon and orange rinds and cinnamon until nearly boiling. Cover and infuse for 10-15 minutes. Remove the fruit rinds and cinnamon and serve sweetened to taste with Hermesetas. Float the orange slices in the punch.

Kaffee Punch

Serves 4

Metric		Imperial
340 (85)	CALORIES	**340 (85)**
1 litre	**hot strong black coffee**	1¾ pints
	Hermesetas Liquid Sweetener to taste	
300 ml	**unsweetened orange juice**	½ pint
6 tablespoons	**Cointreau**	6 tablespoons
8 tablespoons	**Low-calorie Topping (see page 82)**	8 tablespoons
½ teaspoon	**drinking chocolate to sprinkle**	½ teaspoon

Mix together the coffee, Hermesetas, orange juice and Cointreau and divide between four glasses. Carefully float the Low-calorie Topping on the drink and sprinkle with the drinking chocolate before serving.

Mulled Wine Cup

See photograph on page 124
Serves 10

Metric		Imperial
550 (55)	CALORIES	**550 (55)**
1	**small lemon**	1
5	**cloves**	5
1	**small orange**	1
1	**cinnamon stick**	1
$\frac{1}{4}$ teaspoon	**grated nutmeg**	$\frac{1}{4}$ teaspoon
300 ml	**boiling water**	$\frac{1}{2}$ pint
1 bottle	**red Burgundy**	1 bottle
	Hermesetas Liquid Sweetener to taste	

Stud the lemon with the cloves. Place on a baking tray and cook in a moderate oven (180°C, 350°F, Gas Mark 4) for 15 minutes. Pare the rind from the orange, squeeze out the juice and place in a saucepan with the rind, cinnamon, nutmeg and water. Bring to the boil, cover and infuse away from the heat for 30 minutes. Strain into a large saucepan and add the wine and lemon. Heat but do not boil. Add Hermesetas to taste. Serve from a warmed bowl into warmed glasses.

Irish Coffee

See photograph on page 124
Serves 4

Metric		Imperial
240 (60) if whipped cream used	CALORIES	if whipped cream used **240 (60)**
200 (50) if Low-calorie Topping used		if Low-calorie Topping used **200 (50)**
4 tablespoons	**Irish whiskey, warmed**	4 tablespoons
900 ml	**hot strong black coffee**	$1\frac{1}{2}$ pints
	Hermesetas Liquid Sweetener to taste	
8 tablespoons	**lightly whipped cream or Low-calorie Topping** **(see page 82)**	8 tablespoons

Warm four large, strong wine glasses or Irish coffee glasses. Divide the whiskey between them. Put a silver teaspoon in each glass and fill almost to the top with the hot coffee. Add Hermesetas to taste. Float about 2 tablespoons of cream or Low-calorie Topping on each one. Drink the coffee through the cream.

With the advent of the freezer you may think that seasonality of foods is a thing of the past. To some extent it is. But you may want to retain some of the interest in eating by keeping in step with seasonal fruits and vegetables. The selection of menus on the following pages shows combinations of foods that are in season.

Of course, you can serve what you like. But try to contrast textures in a meal so that one course is crisp and another soft. If you need to introduce crispness to a smooth soup or savoury mousse, serve Slimcea Melba Toast as well. Think about colour so that you don't finish up with a white soup, white fish and cauliflower followed by white ice cream. It may taste delicious but it will look extremely boring, and most people are much more concerned about what food looks like than its taste.

The other consideration is, of course, calories. It's usually better to start planning a meal by deciding on the main course. Then you can fit the starter and dessert around that. When you're entertaining friends you should be prepared to relax your diet a little; it's very embarrassing for your guests to eat a hearty three course meal while you play with a plate of cottage cheese. As with everything else, forward planning is the secret.

The menus we've used as examples range from the formal dinner party to less formal family meals, from high to low calorie – but all possible for someone eating 1200 Calories a day.

When you're planning your own meals, don't think you can't use breakfast dishes in the evening, or cakes for desserts. You can please yourself and still enjoy it!

Spring Menus

1

	Calories
Cottage Eggs *page 23*	185
Fish Florentine *page 42*	230
Broccoli spears	20
Malvern Pudding *page 85*	70
TOTAL CALORIES	**505**

2

Salmon salad (lettuce, cucumber and 50 g/2 oz salmon)	80
Spring Chicken *page 47*	230
Jacket baked potato (200 g/7 oz)	200
Sliced green beans	10
Fruit Fool *page 98*	60
TOTAL CALORIES	**580**

3

Golden Vegetable Soup *page 36*	130
Gingered Kidney Casserole *page 63*	180
50 g/2 oz cooked rice	70
50 g/2 oz mixed vegetables	30
Slimmers' Cheesecake *page 100*	110
TOTAL CALORIES	**520**

Summer Menus

1

	Calories
Cucumber and Mint Soup *page 37*	70
Lamb Kebabs *page 56*	410
Whole French beans with mushrooms	20
175 g/6 oz strawberries, raspberries and redcurrants with 3 tablespoons Marvel yogurt	75
TOTAL CALORIES	**575**

2

Wedge of melon	30
Baked chicken quarter with tarragon	230
Tomato and cucumber salad with Slimmers' Yogurt Dressing *page 79*	40
Orange, watercress and onion salad	40
Iced Coffee Sorbet *page 90*	60
TOTAL CALORIES	**400**

3

Greek Lemon Soup *page 38*	70
175 g/6 oz hake steak baked in foil with sliced leeks	160
Baked tomatoes	20
Baked courgettes	20
Italian-style Ice Cream with 100 g/4 oz fresh fruit *page 89*	75
TOTAL CALORIES	**345**

Autumn Menus

1

	Calories
Turkey Pots *page 34*	120
250 g/9 oz grilled Dover sole with small bunch grapes	230
Chicory, sweetcorn and pepper salad	30
Fiesta Pancakes *page 81*	155
TOTAL CALORIES	535

2

Tomato stuffed with cottage cheese and chives	60
Worcestershire Beef *page 56*	230
100 g/4 oz mashed potato	90
100 g/4 oz braised cabbage	40
Rhubarb and Ginger Crisp *page 85*	65
TOTAL CALORIES	485

3

California Prawn Cocktail *page 27*	50
Curried Chicken with Fruit *page 53*	310
100 g/4 oz rice	110
Apricot Sherbet *page 91*	90
TOTAL CALORIES	560

Winter Menus

1

	Calories
Baked egg with 1 tablespoon single cream per egg	120
Crunchy Haddock Casserole *page 40*	255
50 g/2 oz peas and pearl onions	30
Chocolate Whip *page 97*	95
TOTAL CALORIES	500

2

Vegetable Bortsch *page 35*	45
Pork fillet (100 g/4 oz) roasted with prune stuffing	200
Braised celery	20
Lemon Mousse *page 92*	95
TOTAL CALORIES	360

3

Fish Mousse *page 26*	145
Turkey in Mushroom Sauce *page 46*	290
50 g/2 oz Brussels sprouts	30
Baked Ginger Pears *page 82*	75
TOTAL CALORIES	540

Summer Outdoor Menu

	Calories
3 Slimcea Open Sandwiches *page 118*	approx. 300
Patio Dip (quarter of recipe) *page 70*	90
Selection of raw vegetables	30
100 g/4 oz fresh fruit salad	50
TOTAL CALORIES	470

Special Dinner Party Menu

	Calories
Mushroom Cream *page 28*	45
Easy Paella *page 48*	390
Green salad	20
Apple Snow *page 91*	85
Glass dry wine	100
TOTAL CALORIES	640

Speedy Lunch Menu

	Calories
Pipérade with Eggs *page 110*	270
2 slices Slimcea and Outline	125
1 piece fresh fruit	60
TOTAL CALORIES	455

Late Supper Menu

	Calories
Chicken Liver Soup *page 34*	approx. 155
Egg Tartlets *page 112*	240
Greek Cheese Salad *page 78*	130
TOTAL CALORIES	525

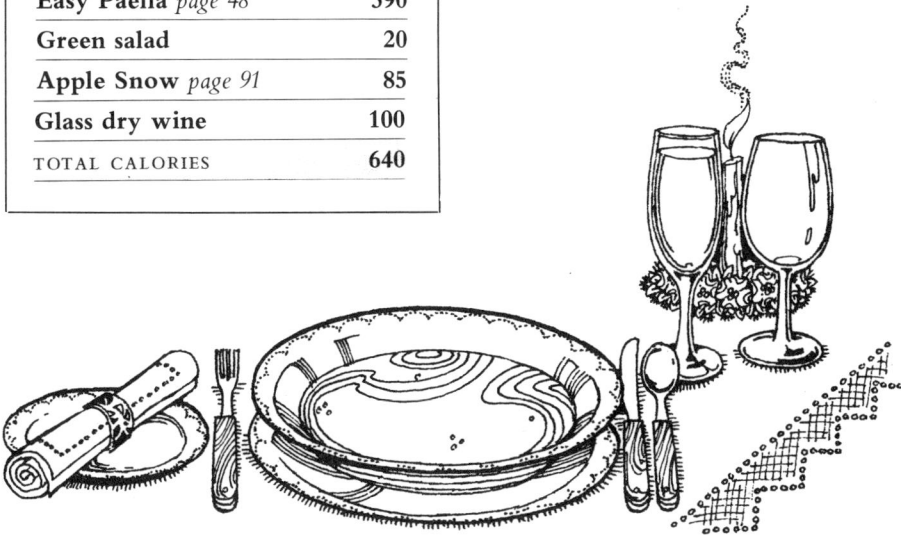

Table 1

A Guide to Ideal Weights

Height without shoes			Desirable weight in kilograms and pounds (in indoor clothing), ages 25 and over					
			Small frame		Medium frame		Large frame	
metres	ft	in	kg	lb	kg	lb	kg	lb
					Men			
1.550	5	1	50.8-54.4	112-120	53.5-58.5	118-129	57.2-64.0	126-141
1.575	5	2	52.5-55.8	115-123	54.9-60.3	121-133	58.5-65.3	129-144
1.600	5	3	53.5-57.2	118-126	56.2-56.7	124-136	59.9-67.1	132-148
1.625	5	4	54.9-58.5	121-129	57.6-63.0	127-139	61.2-68.9	135-152
1.650	5	5	56.2-60.3	124-133	59.0-64.9	130-143	62.6-70.8	138-156
1.675	5	6	58.1-62.1	128-137	60.8-66.7	134-147	64.4-73.0	142-161
1.700	5	7	59.9-64.0	132-141	62.6-68.9	138-152	66.7-75.3	147-166
1.725	5	8	61.7-65.8	136-145	64.4-70.8	142-156	68.5-77.1	151-170
1.750	5	9	63.5-68.0	140-150	66.2-72.6	146-160	70.3-78.9	155-174
1.775	5	10	65.3-69.9	144-154	68.0-74.8	150-165	72.1-81.2	159-179
1.800	5	11	67.1-71.7	148-158	69.9-77.1	154-170	74.4-83.5	164-184
1.825	6	0	68.9-73.5	152-162	71.7-79.4	158-175	76.2-85.7	168-189
1.850	6	1	70.8-75.7	156-167	73.5-81.6	162-180	78.5-88.0	173-194
1.875	6	2	72.6-77.6	160-171	75.7-83.9	167-185	80.7-90.3	178-199
1.900	6	3	74.4-79.4	164-175	78.0-86.2	172-190	82.6-92.5	182-204
					Women			
1.425	4	8	41.7-44.5	92-98	43.5-48.5	96-107	47.2-54.0	104-119
1.450	4	9	42.6-45.8	94-101	44.5-49.9	98-110	48.1-55.3	106-122
1.475	4	10	43.5-47.2	96-104	45.8-51.3	101-113	49.4-56.7	109-125
1.500	4	11	44.9-48.5	99-107	47.2-52.6	104-116	50.8-58.1	112-128
1.525	5	0	46.3-49.9	102-110	48.5-54.0	107-119	52.5-59.4	115-131
1.550	5	1	47.6-51.3	105-113	49.9-55.3	110-122	53.5-60.8	118-134
1.575	5	2	49.0-52.6	108-116	51.3-57.2	113-126	54.9-62.6	121-138
1.600	5	3	50.3-54.0	111-119	52.6-59.0	116-130	56.7-64.4	125-142
1.625	5	4	51.7-55.8	114-123	54.4-61.2	120-135	58.5-66.2	129-146
1.650	5	5	53.5-57.6	118-127	56.2-63.0	124-139	60.3-68.0	133-150
1.675	5	6	55.3-59.4	122-131	58.1-64.9	128-143	62.1-69.9	137-154
1.700	5	7	57.2-61.2	126-135	59.9-66.7	132-147	64.0-71.7	141-158
1.725	5	8	59.0-63.5	130-140	61.7-68.5	136-151	65.8-73.9	145-163
1.750	5	9	60.8-65.3	134-144	63.5-70.3	140-155	67.6-76.2	149-168
1.775	5	10	62.6-67.1	138-148	65.3-72.1	144-159	69.4-78.5	153-173

From "Prevention of coronary heart disease" by the Royal College of Physicians and the British Cardiac Society 1976.

Selection of Slimcea Sandwiches (see page 116); Slimcea Open Sandwiches (see page 118); Patio Dip (see page 70)